Dear Amy

Dear Amy

Making Sense of the Voyage of the Soul

Tom Kay

HAMPTONROADS
PUBLISHING COMPANY, INC.

2/96

4/96

For information write:

Hampton Roads Publishing Co., Inc.
891 Norfolk Square
Norfolk, VA 23502

Or call: (804)459-2453
FAX: (804)455-8907

10 9 8 7 6 5 4 3 2 1

ISBN 1-57174-010-4

Printed on acid-free paper in the United States of America

Bookstore

This book is dedicated
to my mother

Mary D. Kay

Thanks, Mom

Contents

2/96

Foreword

At some time, I think, every father has thoughts about what he would like to tell his children about the mysteries of our existence that he has gleaned for himself in his own life. The author, Tom Kay, has sat down at his computer keyboard and done just this in a highly readable message to his beautiful college-age daughter Amy, whom I have known for most of her life. He begins with a letter from Dad, which is quite moving, reminding many of us busy fathers what we failed to do, and then goes into the many questions that we all have at one time asked about the destiny of our souls and where do we go from here. While it may not have all the answers to the questions that Amy and people like me might ask, it does give us much to think about, and makes for provocative reading. There is a poem for Amy which I found touching. Which her author-father describes as "Your Soul's Voyage in Simple Verse." Simple enough to be understood and to symbolize what a father's love for a daughter should symbolize for all parents.

Jess Stearn

Acknowledgements

It's impossible to write an acknowledgement page! How does one keep score? So many have helped me in different ways over the past 25 years.

I'll start by thanking my wife Judie, my son Timmy, and my daughter Amy for putting up with me all these years. Then there's my brother Bob and his wife Ginger for their moral support.

I greatly appreciate the advice and suggestions of Jess Stearn, Wayne Emily, Gordon-Michael Scallion, Aron Abrahamson, and of course my publishers Bob Friedman and Frank DeMarco and my editor Kathy Grotz.

I received a lot of valuable input from Edgar Evans Cayce, Caroline House Freeman, and her mother, Doris House.

Others who helped me in one way or another, mostly by reviewing the manuscript and encouraging me to "carry on," include David Alexander; the Cordaks, Dorothy and Joe, Janice and Gary; Joe Dunn; Phyllis and Jim Embleton; Bruce McArthur; Sam and Rufus Mosely; Joe Nasi; Carol and Walter Noona; Donna Paxson; Gail Cayce Schwatzer; Richard Ware; and Adella Scott Wilson and her daughter Ayla.

I'm especially indebted to all of the people, past and present, who have been involved with the work of Edgar Cayce. As for *A Course in Miracles*, the ideas presented herein are the author's personal interpretation and understanding of some of the concepts found in the Course, and are not endorsed by the copyright holder of the Course.

Finally, a special thanks to Francine Barbet for taking my simple idea for the cover of the book and turning it into a beautiful work of art.

Dear Amy,

Lately I've been thinking about those "oh so many talks" you and I have had since you were a little girl. You know — the ones about love and forgiveness, right from wrong, and the "meaning of life." And as you also know, I've never said I have all the answers. In fact, the many questions asked by you and your older brother Timmy have helped me more than either of you will ever know. They have made me think and search for answers too.

I remember the time, about a week before Easter, when four-year-old Timmy asked me, "Daddy, is there an Easter bunny?" He seemed to be satisfied with my answer, because he followed with, "Is there a Santa Claus?" Again my explanation seemed to satisfy him; for after a short pause he asked, "Daddy, is there a God and where is He?" Well, I'm still working on that one. I've concluded that learning is an ongoing process. If we don't "seek" there's not much of a chance we will "find."

So I decided to assemble, in as logical an order as possible, the information and supporting references recalling many of those things we've discussed over the years. I know you've heard it all before. All those "sermons"—the dos and don'ts, life and death, God and the World, and the crazy times in which we live. But it never hurts to ponder themes of this nature from time to time.

I also felt moved to write you a "summary" in simple verse that you could refer to when the mood strikes you or when the going gets tough. It's meant to sort of jog your memory and remind you that the real Amy is a spiritual being. So the final chapter of the book is my special poem to you.

The other chapters include quotes from the Bible, metaphysical information, and other sources that you may want to refer to for comparison, understanding, and your own interpretation. In this way, if you want to explore further, you can "look it up," as your mother and I had to admonish you at times. Finally, I've quoted a number of researchers and well-known persons when I felt it added substance. I'm aware that you are familiar with some of this material, but you will also discover a lot of new information and theories I think you will find interesting and unusual.

Trying to tie all of this together is not easy. Much of the subject matter overlaps because a given excerpt may contain information on several levels. But once you've read it, all the pieces of the puzzle should form a meaningful picture.

After all, there isn't much of anything here that can be proved scientifically. It's mostly *belief.* Although there are many books, some of them scholarly, that present a great deal of evidence that reincarnation was an accepted doctrine of ancient Judaism and the early Christian church, no one can prove they lived in previous times. And the prophecies and predictions for the "New Age" will only be proved after the fact. I guess it's a matter of intuition. Does it "feel right" or "make sense?" After reading this material, as I observe world events and experience my own life, does there seem to be a "connection"?

Listed in the bibliography are the titles of many books that you may want to read. They've increased my awareness along with that of many others. However, I don't endorse any as being 100 percent *truth* all of the time. And sometimes, what I could not understand or accept a few years ago now makes more sense.

My hope is that all of this will be of some use to you as you travel life's highways and byways, and I'm sure we will both have many new insights as time goes on. This is simply my attempt at presenting information I've studied that's increased my awareness. So for now, here is my small gift to you; one that you can use as a reminder of how important you are to God.

Perhaps, as I've tried, you'll want to pass your awareness, understanding, and experiences on to others as we all approach the millennium and the birth of the "New Age."

So turn the page and return to our yesteryears. I'm proud of you and your brother. He's a fine young man, and you're a wonderful daughter, and I love you both very "much much."

Love,
Dad

Dear Amy

Making Sense of the Voyage of the Soul

Who Or What Should We Believe?

There are many, many versions of the Old and New Testaments of the Bible. And then, of course, there are other teachings or books that for one reason or another were not accepted by the early Church or subsequently by other Christian denominations. Fourteen of these books are published in as a companion-type Bible known as the *Apocrypha*. In addition, there are the teachings that are accepted as divinely inspired by members of the other world religions.

Today there are many versions of the Bible for sale in religious book stores. Further, there are more than half a dozen Bible programs for use on the computer.

One of the best is the Logos Bible Software which is distributed by Logos Research Systems, Inc. of Oak Harbor, Washington. In a recent company newsletter, "LogosNews," there is an article, part of which is excerpted as follows:

> Why does Logos offer four different Greek texts [Greek being the language of the early translations]? The reasons may or may not be familiar to you. It all revolves around the issue of the missing autographs.
>
> The mystery of the missing autographs may not be a mystery at all. By autograph we mean the original manuscript written by the original author, for example Paul's letter to the Romans written and hand signed by Paul himself. This document was probably passed around so many times that it finally fell apart or got lost among its own copies. The point is, we don't have any known autographs, just copies and copies of copies and the copy machines in those days had legs and could walk.
>
> The manuscripts and their copies spread throughout the

16

known world. Those manuscripts that went north and west became known as the "Byzantine" or "western" texts. Those that traveled south and east became known as "Alexandrian" or "eastern texts". . .

The manuscripts that propagated in the north and west were copied extensively as Christianity spread throughout Europe. The manuscripts in the south on the other hand were copied infrequently and spent centuries in storage. As a result there are many recent (Middle Ages) manuscripts in the west and few ancient (third and fourth century) manuscripts in the east. These eastern manuscripts were re-discovered in the 1800s with the result that nearly every Bible translated since that time has been based on the older eastern manuscripts to the near total abandonment of the western manuscripts of the Middle Ages. Many manuscripts make one text. Collections of manuscripts and manuscript fragments are necessary to put together whole testaments and whole Bibles. . .

Which text is the correct text? Let us be perfectly clear. We don't know!

The newsletter then goes on to describe the different computer software programs available.

I included these excerpts simply to point out that there are differences among Bible scholars, just as there are different teachings and opinions among denominations. And we don't have the original "autographs" or writers to query. And then, of course, there are the many other religions besides Christianity.

So, where is the truth to be found in the different world religions? According to the famous modern-day mystic and seer Edgar Cayce [K-SEE], the most important truth in any religion, and the first law, is the acknowledgement of the One God and the Oneness of all humanity. And further, that each religion has a purpose—a special place in the evolution of the human soul.

But then the question would obviously follow, how do we know Cayce was right? Again, of course, very few can answer for certain that he was. But to help a little, there is documented evidence that he was truly a gifted person.

I'd guess that more than a hundred books have been published about Edgar Cayce, his gift, and his work — some in perhaps a dozen or so languages. And all but one, the first biography, *There is a River,* have been written since his death in January 1945.

His education was limited to completion of the 8th grade, and from what I've learned, it appears that he and his family had it pretty rough. They never had much money, and they were shuffled around from one home to another most of his life. He was labeled a "kook" by many, and a charlatan by others. At times the stigma carried over to members of his family, his close friends, and those who believed in his sincerity and the accuracy of the information that "came through" him.

Well, from what I can tell, he must have had something to contribute, or his popularity wouldn't have grown and expanded over the years. And it took a lot of guts to do what he did! How many people would be willing to lie on a couch twice a day, put themselves in an unconscious, coma-like state for at least thirty minutes, and then give "readings" and answer questions from an unknown source that was hopefully of good intentions and of a higher intelligence? And then he'd have to wait until the stenographer typed it on paper so he could see if he had made a fool of himself!

Also, many of the persons that requested healing readings were desperate. Some had been sent home to die. Everything had been tried by conventional medicine, and no cure had been found. He was their last chance. Not an easy livelihood, and I guess he tried to run from it many times. But each time he did, someone would come knocking at his door asking for help — more than 14,000 times. Fortunately the readings were recorded and are on file at the Cayce library in Virginia Beach.

For many, it's "by their fruits you will know them." The healing, or "physical" readings have been tried with varying degrees of success by professionals. And today, the practice of *holistic medicine*—treating the whole person—body, mind, and spirit—is becoming more widespread in this country and others as people search for alternative healing methods. In a March 1979 article, the *Journal of the American Medical Association* stated: "the roots of present-day holism probably go back 100 years to the birth of Edgar Cayce in Hopkinsville, Kentucky." Also, many persons who have researched the "prophecy" readings point to convincing evidence that some of his many predictions have come to pass. Of course, many others, including most of the critical ones, still await confirmation. More on this later.

I mentioned the first book, the biography *There is a River*, but as you know, there have been many others. Jess Stearn's *The Sleeping Prophet* was on the New York *Times* best-seller list for about a year, and has been translated into several languages. And the doctor of the rich and famous, Dr. Harold J. Reilly, wrote *The Edgar Cayce Handbook for Health Through Drugless Therapy*, which has been popular and helped people since first published in 1975. The following is from a lecture given by Edgar Cayce in 1933, at the age of 56, while in his "awake" state as he attempted to explain his unusual abilities:

It is rather hard to describe something which has become so much a part of me. It is almost trying to describe what my face looks like—I can show you, but I can't tell you. I can tell you some of my experiences and my thoughts in respect to the readings; but as to what a reading is—well, I can only tell you what other people have said about them and the thoughts that have come to me as I have studied the effects created in the minds of those who have received readings.

It wouldn't be an exaggeration to say that I have been in the unconscious state, during which the readings are given, perhaps 25,000 times in the last 31 years. Yet I myself have never heard a single reading. Then how can I describe one to you?

Many people who have never heard a reading have asked me how I knew I could give one. I never did know it—and I don't know it yet—except by taking another person's word for it.

The first step in giving a reading is this: I loosen my clothes—shoelaces, necktie, shirt cuffs, belt—so that I have a perfectly free-flowing circulation. Next I lie down on the couch in my office. If the reading is to be a "physical" one, I lie with my head to the south; if it is to be a "life" reading, my head is to the north, and feet to the south. I myself do not know the reason for this difference in polarization, as the readings themselves called it.

When I am lying comfortably, I put both my hands to my forehead—to the spot where others have told me the third eye is located—and I pray. . .After praying, I wait a few minutes until I receive what might be called the "go" signal; that is, a flash of brilliant white light, sometimes verging upon a golden color. The light is a sign to me that I have made contact. Until I have seen it, I know that I cannot give reading.

After I have seen the light, I move both my hands down to the solar plexus. Then I'm told, my breathing becomes very deep and rhythmic, from the diaphragm. Several minutes go by. When my eyelids begin to flutter closed—having been open but glazed thus far—the conductor knows I am ready to receive the suggestion. He proceeds to give it to me, slowly and distinctly. For example, if it is a physical reading, the name of the person and the address where he or she may be located at the time are given to me. Then there is a pause—sometimes so long a pause, I'm told, that I appear not to have heard the directions. If so, they are given to me again; and after that, I repeat the name and address very slowly, until the body is located and a description of its condition is begun.

This then is how I give a reading. I am entirely unconscious during the whole procedure. When I wake up I feel slightly hungry; just hungry enough, perhaps, for a cracker and a glass of milk.

As to the validity of the information that comes through me when I sleep—this is the question, naturally, that occurs to everyone. Personally, I feel that its validity depends largely upon how much faith and confidence lie within the one who seeks this source of information. Its validity, of course, has been objectively proved many hundreds of times by the results that have come from applying the advice obtained.

In regard to the source of the information, naturally I have some ideas about it. But even though I have been doing this work for thirty-one years, I know very little about it. Whatever I might say would be largely a matter of conjecture. I can make no claims whatsoever to great knowledge, for I am only groping.

But then, we all learn by experience, do we not? We come to have faith and understanding only by taking one step at a time. Most of us don't have the experience of getting religion all at once—like the man who got it halfway between the bottom of the well and the top, when he was blown out by an explosion of dynamite. Most of us need to have experiences and to arrive at conclusions by weighing the evidence along with some that answers from deep within our inner selves.

As a matter of fact, there would seem to be not just one, but several sources of information tapped when I am in this sleeping state. One source, apparently, is the record made by an individual or entity in all of its experiences through what we call time. The sum total of the experiences of that soul is written, so to speak, in the subconscious of that individual as well as what is known as the Akashic records. Anyone may read these records, if one can attune oneself rightly. Apparently, I am one of the few people who may lay aside the personality sufficiently to allow the soul to make this attunement to the universal source of knowledge. I say this, however, not in a boastful way; in fact, I don't claim to possess any power that any other person doesn't possess. I sincerely believe that there isn't any person, anywhere, who doesn't have the same ability I have. I'm certain that all human beings have much greater powers then they are ever aware of—providing they are willing to pay the price of detachment from self-interest, which is required to develop those powers or abilities. Would you be willing, even once a year, to put aside your own personality—to pass entirely away from it?

Now some people think that the information coming through me is given by some departed personality who wishes to communicate, some benevolent spirit or guide from the other side. This may sometimes be true, but in general I am not a 'medium' in that sense of the term. If the person who seeks the reading, however, comes seeking that kind of contact or information, I believe he or she receives that kind.

Many people ask me how I prevent undesirable influences from entering the work I do. In order to answer that question, let me tell an experience I had when I was a child. When I was between eleven and twelve years of age, I had read the Bible through three times. Now I have read it fifty-six times. No doubt, some people have read it more times than that; but I have tried to read it once for each year of my life.

Well, as a child, I prayed that I might be able to do something for other people—to aid them in understanding themselves and especially to aid children in their ills. One day I had a vision which convinced me that my prayer had been heard and would be answered.

So I believe that my prayer is being answered; and as I go into the unconscious condition, I do so with that faith. I also believe that the source of information will be from the Universal, if the connection is not made to waver by the desires of the person seeking the reading.

Of course, if that person's desire is very intense to have a communication from Grandpa, Uncle, or some great soul, then the contact is directed that way and such becomes the source.

Do not think I am discrediting those who seek in such a way. If you're willing to receive what Uncle Joe has to say, that is what you get. If you're willing to depend upon a more Universal Source, then that is what you get.

"What ye ask, ye shall receive" is like a two-edged sword. It cuts both ways.

I think it is important to understand that Cayce was a healer first. Over 8,000 of his recorded readings were given for individuals suffering from a wide variety of physical ailments. In the final section of the first Cayce biography, *There is a River* (the title chosen from the 46th Psalm) by Thomas Sugrue, there are six case histories typical of his healing abilities. Few people knew Edgar Cayce or his readings better than Sugrue. I've chosen one case that I feel illustrates the exceptional Cayce gift while at the same time demonstrating the procedure and results. To further add to this marvel is the fact that most readings, as with this one, were given for individuals that were hundreds or even thousands of miles removed from the location where Cayce was giving the reading itself. The distance from the reading location didn't seem to matter.

Once Cayce "went under," the suggestion was given to him. It would go something like this: "You will have before you (name)—[now numbers in the public library files for privacy reasons]—born (date of birth) at (place of birth) and presently located at (street address, city and state). You will give the physical condition of this body at the present time, with suggestions for corrective measures; answering the questions, as I ask them."

The reading would then commence, and here we pick up the story from our selected case history, told through the correspondence.

Sept. 25, 1939.

Mr. Edgar Cayce
Virginia Beach, Va.

Dear Mr. Cayce:
Sometime ago, I read an article in the magazine *Health Culture,* on the wonderful work you have been doing for the past twenty-five years, diagnosing diseases through the subconscious mind. The article was from the pen of Dr. Thos. Garrett, N.Y.

The article was like a ray of hope for me.

Briefly my case is this.

For the past twenty-five years, since my ordination to the priesthood in the Catholic Church, I have been engaged in the work of young missions.

About fifteen years ago, while at the altar, I suffered an attack that had all the appearances of epilepsy. There is no epilepsy to my knowledge in our family.

About every three to four years since that time, I have had (at the altar in all cases but one) a similar attack.

You can understand life under these circumstances is very trying, uncertainty of never knowing when an attack will come on makes life very trying. I feel like one caught in a trap. The attack is always preceded by a trembling of the hands and body, which I cannot control. Then follows a period of unconsciousness.

Knowing of the amazing gift which is yours, I am asking you to diagnose and cure my case.

Will you let me know what offering I can give you? I

have very little money but will give what I can.

The article by Dr. Garrett has given me such hope. Will you kindly answer this letter at your earliest convenience? An early answer would be greatly appreciated by one who had been a constant sufferer from fear these past years.

Sincerely yours,

—————

Sept. 27, 1939.

Dear [name]—

I have yours of the 25th and sincerely hope that with His help I may be of a service to you. Thank you for writing me. I trust I may be of a service.

I would not have you pay me anything. I ask that you fill out the enclosed blank or give the information asked for on it, and if you wish to contribute anything say a Mass for my friend, a young Catholic who is in my home trying to regain his health. He was a schoolmate of my son. He is on the improve, slowly but surely, and is a lovely and competent young man.

I am sending you some data, Father. I hope you will enjoy reading it. I will appreciate any comment you may make.

Only two readings can be given each day. The time we have set for yours is the morning of the 6th of Oct., 10:30 to 11:30 EST. We ask that, if practical, you keep the hour in prayerful meditation. Please let me know if it is convenient for you to keep that hour.

Thanking you and sincerely hoping to be of a service, and asking that you remember me in your prayers, I am

Sincerely yours,
EDGAR CAYCE

September 30, 1939.

Dear Mr. Cayce:

Your most welcome and cordial letter, together with the readings and case histories reached me this morning.

God has endowed you with an amazing power. I am seeking that power sincerely in the hope that by a permanent cure, I may be able to give my whole life to the work of helping humanity to a better knowledge of God. This has been my work through twenty-five years in the priesthood, young Catholic Missions, trying to lead people to God.

Let me thank you sincerely for your kindness in making me an Associate Member free of charge in the Association for Research and Enlightenment. Rest assured I will say Mass for your good friend. Rest assured also, Mr. Cayce, I will say Mass for you, and pray for you, to the end that God may give you through your truly wonderful faculty, the power to restore me and others to good health and better appreciation of life's purpose.

On the morning of October 6th, I will spend the hour from 10:30 to 11:30 EST. in prayerful meditation. This is the hour you have set aside for my reading.

May God bless you. You have my sincere prayers and belief in your great work.

Sincerely yours,

—————

The reading was given on the morning of October 6, 1939. The major portion of this reading follows:

Yes, we have the body here [name]—

As we find, the general physical forces are very good in many respects; yet there are disturbances at times which prevent the normal reactions in the body.

These, as will be seen, arise under conditions where strain is brought on the physical forces of the body, — through the very necessity of the period of consecration.

This is a physical condition that, as we find, may be

removed or eliminated; and thus removing from the system the causes of these disturbances, also removing the necessity or cause for fear of ANY nature in relationship to same.

In times back, there were periods when there was a depletion of the physical forces through the lack of supplying full nutriment to the system. This caused, in those areas about the lacteal and umbilical plexus, a form of lesion, —a tautness.

Not that it affects, as yet, the liver or the spleen, or even the gall duct's activity; though eventually, without its removal, it may cause disturbances through that area.

But with the periods of activity in which there is the refraining from foods, this becomes a retroactive condition in the physical force of the body; thus producing a spasmodic reaction in the nerve forces about the area, —causing a reaction through the sympathetic and cerebrospinal center, from the lower portion of the solar plexus center.

Thus there is an inclination for the losing of control of the sensory forces; for it produces, from the reaction, a condition at the 1st cervical, or through the medulla oblongata, —an unbalancing, as it were, of the reflexes to the sensory centers.

This as we find also produces in the general elimination system the inclinations at times for the lack of proper or full eliminations.

When there has been, and is, the better or perfect accord in this direction, there is not such a great stress upon this disturbance in the right portion of the upper abdomen, —as had been indicated, —about the umbilical and lacteal duct center. Here we would find, upon examination, a COLD spot.

In making applications for eradicating the causes, then:

We would apply each evening, for two evenings, the heavy Castor Oil Packs; at least three thicknesses of heavy flannel, wrung out in Castor Oil, as hot as the body can stand same, and placed over the lower portion of the liver, gall duct and caecum area, —this extending, of course, to the umbilical center. Let these remain for one hour at each application, keeping the Packs hot by wringing out of the hot Castor Oil two or three times during the application.

After the two days of applying the Packs, we would

begin then with the osteopathic adjustments, —with particular reference to subluxation as will be found indicated in the lower portion of the 9th dorsal center, or 9th, 10th and 11th. Co-ordinate such correction with the lumbar axis and the upper dorsal and cervical centers.

There should not be required more than six adjustments to correct the condition.

Two of the Castor Oil Packs should be sufficient, but if in the administration of the adjustments it is found that this has NOT relaxed nor removed the cold spot, then apply the Pack again.

Then, be mindful that there are good eliminations, or a perfect or full evacuation of the alimentary canal each day.

When necessary, use a vegetable compound as a laxative, —such as [brand name]— or that having a senna base.

These done, in the manners indicated, will eradicate the causes of the disturbance, and produce throughout the physical forces of the body a better and a nearer normal reaction.

Keep that attitude of consistent help, aid for others. This is in keeping with the purposes, the desires, the heart of the entity.

We are through for the present.

October 9, 1939.

Dear [name]—
I hope you find the information interesting and the suggestions as beneficial as so many hundreds have found them through the years. I do not know how to thank you for your letter. I can assure you that you have brought joy to the young man here, as well as to myself. We can only hope your experience with the information will be as helpful as our own has been.

I will appreciate hearing from you. Thanking you and trusting to have been of some service, I am

Sincerely,
EDGAR CAYCE.

October 11, 1939.

Dear Mr. Cayce:

Your reading and the suggestions for cure, also your personal letter came to me today. Thank God, and you through whom God is working, after all these years I have got, through your aid, at the root of the trouble and have had the remedies pointed out to me.

The osteopathic treatments can be secured here in [location]. I am just at a loss to know how to go about the application of the Castor Oil Packs. They should be applied by one who has a scientific knowledge of the areas mentioned in your reading. To go to a doctor here, who does not understand or who has no knowledge of your truly amazing power, would mean a refusal.

If you could suggest someone, who could apply those packs scientifically without the necessity of my going to a medical doctor, it would indeed solve my problem. I am so anxious to start the treatments at once.

I said Mass this morning for your good friend. I am saying Mass for you tomorrow that God may grant you many years of usefulness to mankind.

May I thank you again for your great kindness to me. I shall never forget you.

Sincerely,

———————

October 14, 1939.

Dear [name]—

Thank you for yours of the 11th. Let me tell you how appreciative my friend is for your saying Mass for him. I thank you also for your thoughtfulness of me.

Now don't think you have need to be disturbed about the Castor Oil Packs. You can apply them more scientifically than anyone else. This is what you do. First get a large piece of flannel, such as part of a blanket. Have it sufficiently large so that when folded three times it will cover the area from the lower portion of your right rib to the point of the hip on the same side and to the center of the abdomen and half round the right side to the spine. Heat sufficient oil so that you can wring the folded cloth out in it. When the oil gets very warm it is messy. Then, after wringing out the flannel in the oil, apply it directly to the body. Have other cloths and a piece of oilcloth to cover the flannel, so that it may not spoil the bed clothing. Apply it as warm as you can stand it. Then turn on your electric pad, and lie still for the time indicated. I am sure you can do this.

Where this treatment has been recommended it has been most effective and I am sure it will prove so for you. When you are ready to take the Oil Pack off, sponge the area covered by oil with a little warm soda water. This cleanses very nicely.

If I haven't been explicit enough, please don't hesitate to ask me about it.

You know I will be anxious to hear how you come along with the osteopath.

We can give the osteopath many references here in the states if he wishes them.

Thank you again. I hope that I have been of help in His name.

Sincerely,
EDGAR CAYCE

December 18, 1939.

Dear Mr. Cayce:
I am so happy to report to you that I have taken the treatments indicated in your reading for my case. Today I finished my sixth osteopathic treatment. The osteopath thinks several more adjustments are necessary to fully restore my body to complete normalcy.

My Christmas greetings to you are these. May God spare you many more years to carry on the good work. I am deeply grateful to you for your kindness. I am sure as I read (and I do often) your letter (my reading) that now I can go on in the full hope that there will be no reoccurrence of the attacks that have made each day an uncertain problem.

Since I began this letter, I have received your lovely Christmas greeting. God bless you with continued health and usefulness. Merry Christmas to you and your family and a happy New Year.

Sincerely,

_____

December 20, 1939.

Dear [name]—

Thank you for yours of the 18th. To feel that I may have been privileged to be the channel for some help or aid to you, is indeed a real Christmas to me, and I can only give humble thanks for this opportunity. I sincerely hope you took sufficient of the Oil Packs to break up the adhesions which were described as the basis of the trouble. With this accomplished, the adjustments from the osteopath will really be more helpful.

I am enclosing two pieces of work by my friend. He is still with us, and is looking forward to having his wife and baby with him tomorrow through Christmas Day. He is very happy about this, to be sure. Slowly but surely he is improving, and if it be His will he will continue until he is again in normal health. He is capable of making so may people happy through his work.

Thanking you for your prayers and blessings, and wishing that all that is good and true be yours, I am

Sincerely,
EDGAR CAYCE

On April 25, 1941, a request was made for a report on the case. The following letter was received with the case report.

April 28, 1941.

Dear Mr. Cayce:

I am just in receipt of your letter. Let me state that I am sure my cure is permanent. To say I am grateful to you is only half stating my feelings. I pray for you daily that God may extend your life into many years to be of service to mankind.

I did not write chiefly for two reasons. First, I wished the element of time to prove my cure was permanent. Second, I was engaged in war work that precluded many times the possibility of correspondence.

It must be a source of great comfort to you to know you are doing so much good for humanity. Let me tell you, I will never forget your kindness to me. May God bless you always.

Sincerely,

Interesting reading, but there are thousands more in the files. The many readings Cayce gave for psoriasis, for example, have been well documented and published by Dr. John O. A. Pagano. This illustrated report reveals, for the first time, a new drug-free approach to conquering one of mankind's oldest skin diseases. The "before and after" pictures in this book are startling!

As another example, I know of several people who have tried the Cayce remedy for arthritis of the joints by massaging the affected area with a combination of peanut and olive oil, with good results.

You have known our good friend, Mrs. Caroline House Freeman, all of your life. But I don't think she ever told you that she was a "Cayce baby" and that he healed her from terrible burns she suffered as a baby. Her grandfather was Thomas Burr House, M.D. He was the staff doctor at the Cayce Hospital in Virginia Beach when it was in operation prior to the Great Depression of the 1930s.

The House family was living in Hopkinsville, Kentucky, at the time. She had five readings prior to this one and was assigned I.D. number 2015.

Background of Reading 2015-6 F 1 [Female, age 1]
10/11/40 A.M. Phone request by Mr. Thomas House.

Caroline pulled over a pan of boiling water onto her face, stomach and feet—all burned very badly; Dr. Gaither [Gant Gaither, M.D.] thinks one eye is burned.

2015-6

Text of Reading 2015-6 F 1

This Psychic Reading given by Edgar Cayce at his home on Arctic Crescent, Virginia Beach, Va., this 11th day of October, 1940, in accordance with request made by the father—Mr. Thomas House, Associate Member of the Ass'n for Research & Enlightenment, Inc.

Present

Edgar Cayce; Gertrude Cayce, Conductor; Gladys Davis, Steno.

Reading

Time of Reading

4:10 to 4:20 P.M. Eastern Standard Time, Hopkinsville, Ky.

Gertrude Cayce: You will give the physical condition of this body at the present time, with suggestions for further corrective measures; answering the questions, as I ask them:

Edgar Cayce: Yes—we have the body here.

While these appear very serious in the present, because of the blister or the water, we do not find the injury to the eyes, but rather to the lids.

As we find, we would cleanse and use the tannic acid; followed with the Unguentine and the Sweet Oil (Camphorated) to prevent or remove scars, as the tissue heals.

Be very mindful that eliminations are kept above the normal. Use BOTH the Podophyllum and the Calomel as a base for eliminants, at various times; not together; but under the direction of the physician. While these would not be used under most circumstances for a child, these would be the better in this case—because of the poisons from so much area covered with the burn, and the shock to the system, as well as the kind of poisons to be eliminated, and the need for the excess lymph.

Ready for questions.

Q: Apply tannic acid?

A: Tannic acid; the light, to be sure; this is understood by the physician. Cleanse it first, then apply the tannic acid.

Q: How should it be cleansed?

A: Would you ask how to tell a doctor to cleanse a thing!

Q: Are they using the tannic acid in the way suggested here?

A: Not using it as yet, but these are a part of the bandages.

Q: Then after the tannic acid apply the Unguentine?

A: As it heals; not, of course, while the tannic acid is being used, but as it heals. See, this cuts away air, produces dead skin, and leaves a scar. Then the Oils from the Unguentine, and the Sweet Oil and the Camphorated Oil are to take away scar tissue, see? These are to follow within ten days to two weeks, see?

Q: The eyes themselves are not injured?

A: As indicated, the lids; though there will be, of course, some inflammation. But keep down the excesses of poisons by increasing the eliminations, to remove these poisons that are as natural accumulations from such an area burned.

Q: Any suggestions for relieving the pain?

A: As just given, this will relieve the pain when it cuts off the air!

We are through for the present.

Copy to Parents, Air Mail
" " Ass'n file.

[10/11/40 Gladys Davis's note: Wired Day Letter as follows:

CLEANSE THEN USE LIGHT TANNIC ACID BANDAGES INCREASE ELIMINATIONS BY PODOPHYLLUM OR CALOMEL BASE UNDER PHYSICIAN'S DIRECTIONS EYES NOT INJURED ONLY LIDS FULL INFORMATION AIR MAIL.]

Reports of Reading 2015-6 F 1

10/18/40 Mother's card: "Baby getting along find—tho' far from being out of the woods as yet. So grateful for reading!—it was the first thing I thought of when I saw what had happened—She's so well & healthy (thanks again to the readings) that she's responding rapidly to her treatment. Don't think her face will be scarred, and so thankful for her eyes.

"Will write soon all the details—Love to each of you. . ."

10/19/40 Father's letter to Edgar Cayce:
"Just want to write you and thank you for the Reading. We have followed it to the letter and you should see the response we have gotten. Caroline has improved 100% and her little face has entirely cleared up without leaving any sign of scar.

"We got a good scab over her little body and arm with the Tannic Acid. Then yesterday the scab started coming off and we cut it away a little at a time as it loosened up. We found that the burns are healing nicely under the scabs. For the last couple of days she has been itching pretty badly and she didn't sleep much last night as a result of this. However she is asleep now and has been for several hours. Didn't even wake up for her supper tonight. Dr. Dade [Randolph Dade, M.D.] has marveled at the way she has responded to the treatment. He has followed the treatment outlined in the Reading with the exception of the Podophyllum. Said he considered it too strong for her and the way she was responding to treatment she did not need it. He used the Calomel however with excellent results. . ."

Recently, I discussed this incident with Mrs. Freeman's mother, Mrs. Doris House. Briefly, she told me that their family doctor had mentioned to her husband that the burns were so severe that it might be better if baby Caroline didn't survive because she would be horribly scarred all her life.

Without a doubt, this didn't happen. Mrs. Freeman even did them one better. She was such an attractive young lady that she was twice chosen as the winner of regional beauty contests.

Of course, many of the readings concerned subjects other than healing. Some were for personal or business guidance; others concerned the interpreting of dreams. Lots of seekers sought guidance about the development of psychic abilities because some wanted to learn to rely on their own hidden intuition or *psychic* (from the Greek, meaning "of the soul") capabilities rather than those of Cayce or others that claimed to have a similar talent.

There were readings on prophecy, world affairs, and of course the "meaning of life." Thousands of questions were asked in order to hopefully achieve a better understanding of the teachings and history of the Bible.

In the middle 1920s, the first hint that there might be something to the proposition of reincarnation was spoken by Edgar Cayce in a "meaning of life" reading.

Edgar Cayce's youngest son, Edgar Evans Cayce, a retired engineer living in Virginia Beach, told me:

> When Dad awakened from the reading and was told he mentioned a past life of the individual asking all of these philosophical questions, he was dumbfounded. He knew as little about reincarnation as he knew about medicine. He was well versed in Christianity and the Bible, but he had never studied other world religions. Abstract questions of philosophical systems had never concerned him. He was awash in waves of doubt about this new information from his unconscious. He was what today would be called a fundamentalist Christian, attended Church regularly, and was an excellent Sunday school teacher of the Bible.

So it seems that when the reincarnation information first surfaced as representing part of the "system" in which human souls function, Edgar Cayce was worried that he had tapped into an unreliable source.

But from that point on, he had persistent questions on the subject. One reading on the issue simply said "you can read reincarnation into the Bible or out of it!" And in his waking state, he never tried to sell anyone on the issue. Many times he would advise people (as the readings would from time to time) to "leave it alone" if it didn't feel right.

The Cayce readings are at times difficult to understand and interpret. The language used can be vague and awkward. And because he read *The King James Version* of the Bible just about every day, while in trance when giving a reading on religious or spiritual matters, he would often use the "thee," "thy," "thou," "ye," "hath," etc. words. As his son Hugh Lynn so aptly explained, "Grammatical confusion and peculiar selection of words and phrases frequently obscure the meaning of the passages in Mr. Cayce's readings. Also, as was the tradition, the term *man* is often used when referring to all of humanity."

The following is a good example of the guidance that came through him concerning spiritual or religious matters:

> Q: What present printed version of the Bible gives the nearest to the true meaning of both Old and New Testaments?
>
> A: The nearest true version for the entity is *that you apply* of whatever version you read *in your life.* . . .There have been many versions of that which was purposed to have been written, and has changed from all those versions. But remember that the whole Gospel of Jesus Christ is "Thou shalt love the Lord thy God with all thy mind, thy heart and thy body; and thy neighbor as thyself. Do this and thou shalt have eternal life." The rest of the book is trying to describe that. It is the same in any language, in any version. (2072-14)

The first statement concerning reincarnation was offered "out of the blue" in a reading for a business man in Dayton, Ohio. It was offered without any suggestion or question on the subject. Cayce, while in a trance, simply stated regarding this person: "Insofar as this entity is concerned, this is the third appearance on this plane, and before this one, as the monk. We see glimpses in the life of the entity now as we were shown in the monk, in his mode of living. The body is only the vehicle ever of that spirit and soul that waft through all times and ever remain the same." (487-1)

This simple statement was the beginning for Edgar and those close to him to commence "past life" investigation. It eventually led to the many requests by individuals seeking information on their previous earth lives. This type of psychic information became known as "life readings."

As Cayce was grappling with the reincarnation information that was so foreign to him, he may have wondered what other surprises were in store for him that were not part of his waking awareness or religious beliefs and conclusions.

Well, if he did wonder, he wouldn't be disappointed. For it wasn't long after the reincarnation predicament emerged that statements in readings of a historical nature began to surface about a small community in the holy land occupied by a deeply religious people known as the Essenes [Es-eens].

The information about this monk-like sect was most likely completely foreign to him. During his time, information about the Essenes was obscure. They were known, however, to a few ancient writers such as Pliney, Philo, and Josephus. In his book *Edgar Cayce's Story of Jesus*, author and researcher Jeffrey Furst states: "Cayce himself had no conscious knowledge of this pre-Christian sect."

But today, since the discovery in 1947 of The Dead Sea Scrolls, a large collection of biblical manuscripts that had been hidden in caves near Jerusalem more than nineteen hundred years ago, much of what Cayce said about the Essenes is being substantiated. A number of researchers involved with the study and translations of the scrolls credit the Essenes with recording many of the scrolls and with playing an important role in the historical exhibits. The remote Essene community was located in the vicinity of the ruins of Qumran where many of the scrolls were discovered.

The Cayce readings of more than fifty years ago, years before the Scrolls were discovered, claimed that the term *Essenes* meant "expectancy" among members of the sect. In the reading numbered 262-61 we find: "Isn't it rather that there were those that ye hear little or nothing of in thy studies, the Essenes—who dedicated their lives, their minds, their bodies to a purpose. . .to them a promise of old. Were there not individuals—men and women—who dedicated their bodies that they might be channels through which such influences, such a body [Jesus] might come?"

In their well-researched and documented book *The Dead Sea Scrolls Deception,* authors Michael Baigent and Richard Leigh have assembled a great deal of reference material and data about the political and religious controversy that has surrounded the scrolls. As with most information that deals with translations from historic manuscripts, especially those of a religious nature, there are as many explanations and opinions concerning interpretation as there are noses on the faces of the scholars and researchers involved.

In their book they quote from the "Biblical Archaeology Review" (BAR): "Referring to Jesus' imminent birth, Luke (1: 32-35) speaks of a child who will be called 'Son of the Most High' and 'Son of God.' The Qumran fragment from Cave 4 also speaks of the coming of someone who 'by his name shall. . .be hailed [as] the Son of God and they shall call him Son of the Most High.' This, as BAR points out, is an extraordinary discovery; the first time that the term 'Son of God' has been found in a Palestinian text outside the Bible."

Cayce gave many readings in which the Essenes were involved and responded to hundreds of questions about the sect. He said both Jesus and John the Baptist were members of the Essenes. Baigent and Leigh, in referencing an article from the New York *Times* quote the following: "The origins of some Christian ritual and doctrines can be seen in the documents of an extremist Jewish sect that existed for more than 100 years before the birth of Jesus Christ. This is the interpretation placed on the 'fabulous' collection of Dead Sea Scrolls by one of an international team of seven scholars. . .John Allegro. . . said last night in a broadcast that the historical basis of the Lord's Supper and part at least of the Lord's prayer and the New Testament teaching of Jesus were attributable to the Qumranians."

We also find quoted in this book: "If, in any case, we look now at Jesus in the perspective supplied by the scrolls, we can trace a new continuity and, at last, get some sense of the drama that culminated in Christianity. . .The monastery [of Quamran]. . .is perhaps, more than Bethlehem or Nazarath, the cradle of Christianity."

Is there also validity in the Cayce readings that supported the doctrine of reincarnation? Will scholars, researchers, and theologians one day conclude that reincarnation is part of the Universal plan for the soul?

There are thousands of supportive books and articles on the subject. It would take a person years to read just the ones available in the library section of the Cayce foundation.

Further, today there are a large number of psychiatrists and psychologists who hypnotize their patients and regress them for therapeutic purposes. Of course, hypnosis has been used for many years to help a person attempt to recall an event in their present life that may have created the problems that finally motivated them to seek professional help. But in many instances, this didn't always achieve curative results. Thus, as a few pioneering doctors searched for other methods, it became a more and more popular treatment to regress patients further back in time, past their present-life birth experiences, and to explore the repressed record of the souls.

One such person, Dr. Brian L. Weiss, M.D., has written two books relating his experiences with past life regression therapy. He is a graduate of Columbia University and Yale Medical School and former chairman of Psychiatry at Mount Sinai Medical Center in Miami, Florida.

Quoting from the publisher, Simon & Schuster, describing his second book, *Through Time Into Healing:* "Dr. Weiss sheds new light on the extraordinary healing potential of regression therapy, based on his extensive clinical experience. Building on time-tested techniques of psychotherapy, he illustrates how, by opening new doors through space and time, past life regression permits the healing of traumas whose roots are to be found not in the present but in a prior lifetime."

I am aware that none of this can be scientifically proven, even if the results are extraordinary in nature. I think it is also important to point out that an enormous number of people now claim to be psychics with the ability to "channel" information and to "read the record of the soul" and interpret the soul's archives. For the most part, they are in my opinion very suspect, not only when excavating this territory, but in their other advice, predictions, and pronouncements. More on this later. As I previously stated, there are a few, both past and present, that I feel deserve serious consideration.

It is well known that the majority of human beings on our planet that "believe in God" also accept the reincarnation doctrine as an important part of the System in which they place their belief. Most of course are connected in some way with the Eastern religions.

But as we now move on to investigate and explore this proposition that has caused so much confusion and controversy, I think you may see that there is much more to the story than first meets the eye.

Reincarnation—
The Absolute Equalizer

Back in the days of the Old West, the availability of the six-shooter gun was widespread. Many individuals carried this weapon because they believed that regardless of their stature or physical strength, it placed them on equal ground with others with whom they came in contact. Thus the six shooter became known as the "great equalizer."

As you will see, based on Creation's Laws and the way they work in the scheme of the reincarnation doctrine, harming another, or taking another's life, regardless of the weapon used can cause a lot of problems and suffering for the "doer of the deed."

For with the doctrine of reincarnation, the equalizer is known as *karma*—a word that many identify with the Buddhist or Hindu religions. Some say that karma is the determining factor in one's fate or destiny.

In today's world the popular saying "what goes around comes around" is often used, but in most cases it is used as a philosophical statement that refers only to the actions of individuals and the results or "rebound" from those same actions in their present, not a past life on earth.

For those members of the Christian and Jewish religions who believe in reincarnation, the usage of the term *karma* is also very common. They like to refer to the many passages in both the New and Old Testaments that they claim confirm their conviction as to the truth of this doctrine.

I suppose the most quoted passage is from the New Testament. In Paul's letter to the Galatians (6:7) he writes: "Make no mistake about this: God is not fooled; a man reaps what he sows."

Also, there is the passage from the Old Testament Book of Job (4:8) that many like to reference: "This I know, that those who plow mischief and sow trouble reap as they have sown."

And there's the "live by the sword, die by the sword" (but not necessarily in the same lifetime) from the book of Revelation (13:10) that many like to point to as alluding to the laws of reincarnation and karma and thus an example of God's perfect justice: "He that leadeth into captivity shall go into captivity; he that killeth with the sword must be killed with the sword. Here is the patience and the faith of the saints."

Also, from Matthew 26:52, Jesus, as he is about to be arrested at Gethsemane, tells one of his defenders who had just cut off the ear of a servant of the high priest, "Put up your sword. All who take the sword die by the sword."

The first question regarding reincarnation that needs to be explored is the "pre-existence" of the soul. Did the soul exist with its mind and free will *before* it entered a physical body (even if there is only one earth life) and therefore occupies the flesh body at birth? Or is the soul of each human created at physical birth with both the conscious and subconscious mind along with free will at the instant it draws its first breath?

Besides the Cayce readings, there are many books that discuss reincarnation and the role it may have played in ancient Judaism and the early Christian Church. One of the more interesting and authoritative ones was written by Joseph Head and S.L. Cranston, entitled *Reincarnation, An East-West Anthology.* As an anthology it mainly consists of quotations from scholars, researchers, and writers of the world's religions plus those of more than 400 western thinkers. The book's "acknowledgments" section contains hundreds of supportive references. Some of what you are about to read are excerpts from this book. A lot of the information is condensed, but I have done my best to preserve the intention and the meaning of it all. You can always get the book and check it out for yourself. First, regarding pre-existence of the soul:

In the early centuries of the Christian era the leading churchmen held varying opinions as to the origin of the soul.

St. Clement of Alexandria (A.D. 150-220), in his *Exhortation to the Pagans* writes: "We were in being long before the foundation of the world; we existed in the eye of God, for it is our destiny to live in Him. . ."

From St. Jerome's (A.D. 340-420) summary of these

views, it is evident all but one involves some form of pre-existence: "As to the origin of the soul, I remember the question of the whole church: whether it be fallen from heaven, as Pythagoras (582-507 B.C.) and the followers of Plato (427-347 B.C.) and Origen (A.D. 185-254) believe. . . or whether they are daily made by God and sent into bodies. . ."

In his 94th Epistle to Avitus, St. Jerome agrees with Origen as to the interpretation [supporting pre-existence of the soul]. . . In the passage mentioned by Origen in *De Principiis*—from Paul's letter to the Ephesians (1:4)— "Who has chosen us before the foundations of the world." Origen concludes, "Every soul. . .comes into this world strengthened by the victories or weakened by the defeats of its previous life. Its place in this world as a vessel appointed to honor or dishonor, is determined by its previous merits or demerits."

Although most have heard of Plato, few are familiar with Origen. Head and Cranston explain:

The *Encyclopedia Britannica* states that Origen was "the most prominent of all Church Fathers with the possible exception of Augustine," while St. Jerome at one time considered him "the greatest teacher of the Church after the Apostles." St. Gregory of Nyssa (A.D. 257-332) called him "the prince of Christian learning in the third century."

Quoting St. Gregory on the subject of reincarnation: "It is absolutely necessary that the soul should be healed and purified, and if it does not take place during its life on earth it must be accomplished in future lives."

As for St. Augustine (A.D. 354-430) on the subject: "The message of Plato, the purest and most luminous in all philosophy has at last scattered the darkness of error, and now shines forth mainly in Plotinus (A.D. 205-270) [who is] so like his master [Plato] that one would think they lived together, or rather—since so long a period of time separates them—that Plato is born again in Plotinus."

Plotinus was a fellow-disciple with Origen under Ammonius,

who founded the famous Alexandrian School of Neo*plato*nism in Egypt in A.D. 193.

It should be pointed out that Augustine later supplanted the doctrine of reincarnation in favor of the doctrine of predestination. He became the most influential theologian of the West, and the father of much that is characteristic of both medieval Catholicism and Protestantism.

There are many other examples of early Church Fathers who openly defended pre-existence of the soul and reincarnation. And there have been many, many more over the centuries and up to the present time who expressed a belief in the doctrine, and, more importantly, that it was in fact accepted by the early church, and by Judaism before the birth of Jesus.

Obviously, Jesus and the Apostles were of the Jewish faith. And, just as today, many denominations or sects were embraced.

Jesus was known as "Rabbi" and Paul, before his conversion, was Saul the Jewish Pharisee. Again quoting from *Reincarnation, An East-West Anthology*: "The ancient Jews were continually expecting the reincarnation of their great prophets. Moses was in their opinion Abel, the son of Adam; and their Messiah was to be the reincarnation of Adam himself. . ."

Did Jesus Himself teach or believe in reincarnation? Was this doctrine one of God's Laws He was referring to when He said He came to fulfill the Law, not change it? And further, did the Apostles and other followers of Jesus also accept it as valid?

If Jesus and his followers did accept and teach the doctrine of reincarnation, then are there possibly any passages in the New Testament that seem to refer to it?

For Bible passages, many supporters start with the closing words of the Old Testament from the book of Malachi (4:5): "Behold, I will send you Elijah the prophet [a Hebrew Prophet, 9th century B.C.], before the coming of the great day of the Lord. . ." followed by the three references in the first book of the New Testament that appear to point to the fulfillment of this prophecy from Malachi.

In Matthew 16:13-14, Jesus asked his disciples, "Who do men say that the Son of Man is?" They answered, "Some say John the Baptist, others Elijah, others Jeremiah, or one of the prophets." And in Matthew 17:10-13, the Apostles ask Jesus, "Why then do our teachers say that Elijah must come first? He replied, yes, Elijah will come and set every thing right. But I tell you that Elijah has already come, and they failed to recognize him, and worked their will upon him, and in the same way the Son of Man is to suffer at their hands. Then the disciples understood that He meant John the Baptist [who had already been beheaded by the ruler, Herod]."

In the New Testament "Gospel According to John" (1: 19-28) are passages that suggest the hierarchy of at least certain Jewish sects were aware of a representative pattern connected with the return of identifiable historic figures from their religious teachings: "This is the testimony which John [the Baptist] gave when the Jews of Jerusalem sent a deputation [delegation] of priests and Levities to ask him who he was [the Levities, from the Jewish Tribe of Levi, were appointed as assistants to the priests because they demonstrated a special zeal for and devotion to the God of Israel]. He confessed without reserve and avowed, 'I am not the Messiah.' 'What then? Are you Elijah?' 'No', he replied. 'Are you the prophet we await?' He answered 'No.' 'Then who are you?' they asked. 'We must give an answer to those who sent us. What account do you give of yourself.' He answered in the words of the prophet Isaiah: [40:3] 'I am a voice crying aloud in the wilderness, make straight the way of the Lord.'"

Earlier, in Matthew 11:11-15, Jesus says: "I tell you this, never has there appeared on earth a mother's son greater than John the Baptist. . .and John is the destined Elijah, if you will but accept it. If you have ears, then hear."

Then the question arises: why would such an exalted soul have to suffer at the hands of Herod?

This may be another example of the law of karma, "what you sow, you shall reap," in the reincarnation scenario. For we read in the Old Testament Book of Kings (18:40) that Elijah had the wicked priests of Baal slain [beheaded?]; all 450 of them!

Another example of the law of karma many point to is from the ninth chapter of John: "As He went on his way Jesus saw a man blind from his birth. His disciples put the question, 'Rabbi, who sinned, this man or his parents? Why was he born blind?' 'It is not that this man or his parents sinned,' Jesus answered, 'he was born blind so that God's power might be displayed in curing him." Jesus then went on to heal the blind man.

Did the disciples have the idea of reincarnation and karma in mind when they questioned Jesus? For obviously if the man had been born blind, his sin could not have been committed in this, his present life. Also, were the disciples speculating that there was some sort of karmic connection between the parents and blind man?

In *Reincarnation, An East-West Anthology,* we find:

> There has never been a papal encyclical [letter of instruction by the Roman Catholic Church] against reincarnation, it would appear. . .The *Catholic Encyclopedia* (Vol. 10, p. 236) states in its article on [reincarnation]:
>
> It was a tenant common to many systems of philosophic thought and religious belief widely separated from each other both geographically and historically. . .There is evidence that at one period or another it has flourished in almost every part of the world. . .This universality seems to mark it as one of those spontaneous or instinctive beliefs by which man's nature responds to the deep and urgent problems of existence. . .but it was too evidently opposed to the Catholic doctrine of *Redemption* to obtain a settled footing.
>
> In the face of a belief at first sight so far fetched and yet at the same time so widely diffused, we are led to anticipate some great general causes which have worked together to produce it. . .
>
> (1) The practically universal conviction that the soul is a real entity distinct from the body and that it survives death;
>
> (2) connected with this there is the imperative moral demand for an equitable future retribution of rewards and punishments in connection with good or ill conduct here. . .

If you feel that a belief in reincarnation does not violate or diminish the teachings of Christianity, you are not alone. Another book that is supportive and thorough on the subject is *Reincarnation in Christianity* by Dr. Geddes MacGregor. On the back cover there is a short biographical sketch as follows: "Dr. Geddes MacGregor is Emeritus Distinguished Professor of Philosophy at the University of Southern California, and has received numerous awards over the years. He is a fellow of the Royal Society of

Literature, and a recipient of the California Literature Award. . .He came to the United States in 1949 as the first holder of the Rufus Jones Chair in Philosophy and Religion at Bryn Mawr. Listed in Who's Who in America, Europe and London, Dr. MacGregor is the author of over twenty books."

Pretty good credentials! The publisher goes on to state: "The question that bothered Dr. Macgregor was quite basic: Can a Christian believe in reincarnation and still remain loyal to the Bible? He decided to find some answers. He researched into the annals of Christian history—cut through centuries of religious emotionalism—gathered his material together and reported his findings in this landmark work. . ."

It also quotes recommendations from members of the Christian clergy concerning the conclusions supporting reincarnation in Dr. MacGregor's book, including Timothy Cardinal Manning, Archbishop of Los Angeles—"Professor MacGregor's exciting thesis challenges our traditional orthodoxy"—and Reverend Ernst Gordon, Dean of Chapel, Princeton University—"Rather than his position detracting from the personal nature of the Christian Life, he enhances and enriches it."

In this book also, we find a lot of information about people with whom most are familiar, confirming their acceptance of reincarnation. MacGregor states: "Henry Ford categorically affirmed a belief in reincarnation. There are some indications Napoleon entertained the notion. Certainly, in more recent times, both Lord Dowding, Chief of the Royal Air Force Fighter Command, and the American General George Patton were ardent subscribers to reincarnationist beliefs."

Interestingly, Head and Cranston write that "Napoleon Bonaparte (1796-1821). . .would cry out to his Marshalls, 'I am Charlemagne' [A.D. 742-814, known as Charles the Great—also crowned emperor of the Romans]. . .he is also quoted as saying 'tell the Pope I am keeping my eyes open; tell him that I am Charlemagne, the Sword of the Church, his Emperor, and as such I expect to be treated.'"

The artist Salvador Dali, who recently passed away, and whose paintings have been on display at the National Gallery of Art and throughout the world, reminded me of Napoleon's assertions regarding Charlemagne; Dali claimed: "I am the reincarnation of one of the greatest of all Spanish mystics, St. John of the Cross. I can remember vividly my life as St. John, of experiencing the divine union, of understanding the dark night of the soul of which he writes with so much feeling. I can remember the monastery and I can remember many of St. John's fellow monks."

Some researchers claim that many of our founding fathers were in agreement with the belief in reincarnation and that some were members of secret societies. In his book *America's Secret Destiny,* Robert Hieronimus, Ph.D., writes: "Four of the nation's founders (Washington, Jefferson, Franklin, and Charles Thompson) are alleged to have been Rosicrucians [Ancient Mystic Order Rosae Crucis], and three (Franklin, Jefferson and Adams) are thought to be initiates in the Illuminate order."

It is well documented that many, including Washington and Franklin, were Freemasons and belonged to various Masonic Lodges. Head and Cranston state "In years past, 'The New Age,' the official Masonic organ of the Supreme Council, 33rd degree, in America, has contained numerous articles treating frankly and sympathetically both rebirth and karma."

Hieronimus does an excellent job of documenting the "New Age" beliefs of these and many other founding fathers. For they are the same assemblage that designed the front and reverse sides of the Great Seal of the United States of America which are displayed on the back side of our one dollar bill. The design of the reverse side of the Great Seal is a Pyramid topped off with the "third" or "spiritual" eye; that which is identified with the psychic aptitude of *clairvoyance* such as Edgar Cayce exhibited from time to time when he was awake and conscious.

From the *American Heritage Dictionary:* "Clairvoyance: The supposed power to perceive things that are out of the natural range of human senses, attributed to certain individuals. Acute intuitive insight or perceptiveness."

The Latin phrase beneath the Pyramid, *Novus Ordo Seclorum* in translation means "New Order of the Ages," and the words *Annuit Coeptus* above, "He Has Prospered Our Undertaking."

And it appears that Benjamin Franklin was a sort of New Age evangelist; for he actively encouraged his friends to explore the validity and "enlightenment" concerning reincarnation, even going so far, at the age of twenty-two, to write the epitaph for, what he knew was the inevitable, his personal grave stone. He then would proceed at every opportunity to pass out copies to his friends. The epitaph reads as follows:

THE BODY OF B. FRANKLIN
PRINTER,
LIKE THE COVER OF AN OLD BOOK,
ITS CONTENTS TORN OUT
AND
STRIPPED OF ITS LETTERING AND GILDING,
LIES HERE
FOOD FOR WORMS,
BUT THE WORK SHALL NOT BE LOST,
FOR IT WILL BE AS HE BELIEVED
APPEAR ONCE MORE
IN A NEW AND MORE ELEGANT EDITION
REVISED AND CORRECTED
BY THE AUTHOR

Thomas Paine (1737-1809) was another of the founding fathers who seemed to have the same philosophical convictions. In his book *The Secret Destiny of America* (on which Heironimus amplified and expanded), well-known philosopher and author Manly Palmer Hall states, "Of Thomas Paine it has been said that he did more to win the independence of the colonies with his pen than George Washington accomplished with his sword."

Head and Cranston quote the following from Paine's *The Age of Reason:* "All other arguments apart, the consciousness of existence is the only conceivable idea we can have of another life, and the continuance of that consciousness is immortality. The consciousness of existence, or the knowing that we exist, is not necessarily confined to the same form, nor to the same matter, even in this life."

The following are some supportive quotes from other well known individuals from *Reincarnation, An East-West Anthology:*

Voltaire (1694-1778)

"The doctrine of reincarnation is, above all, neither absurd nor useless. It is not more surprising to be born twice than once. . ."

Thomas Edison (1847-1931)

"The only survival I can conceive is to start a new earth cycle again." [Edison was one of the early members of the first reincarnationist associations in the West, The Theosophical Society.]

Henry Ford (1863-1947)

"When I was a young man I, like so many others, was bewildered. I found myself asking the question. . .'What are we here for'. . .without some answer to that question life is empty. . . I adopted the theory of reincarnation when I was twenty-six. . . religion offered nothing to the point. . .Even work could not give me complete satisfaction. Work is futile if we cannot utilize the experience we collect in one life in the next. When I discovered reincarnation it was as if I had found a universal plan. I realized that there was a chance to work out my ideas. I was no longer a slave to the hands of a clock. . .The discovery of reincarnation put my mind at ease. . .If you preserve a record of this conversation, write it so it puts men's minds at ease. I would like to communicate to others the calmness that the long view of life gives to us. Genius is experience. Some seem to think it is a gift or a talent, but it is the fruit of long experience in many lives."

William Randolph Hearst (1863-1951)

In one of his daily columns, Hearst wrote: "The architecture of this town [San Miguel de Allende, near Monterrey, Mexico] is particularly striking. Singularly enough, most of it was designed and constructed by Severino Gutierrez, an Indian who had no training or technical knowledge and who drew all his plans with a stick in the sand. Reincarnation may be a fantastic theory, but this Indian genius could not have inherited an amazing talent which none of his ancestors possessed. How then, could he have acquired it except by personal experience in some previous existence?"

Harry Houdini (1874-1926)

The great "escape artist," whose name has become synonymous with extraordinary feats, remarks in an interview: "I firmly believe, and this belief is based on investigation, observation, and in a measure, personal experience—that somehow, somewhere, and sometime, we return in another human form, to carry on, as it were, through another lifetime, perhaps through many succeeding lifetimes, until some strange destiny is worked out to its ultimate solution. . ."

Albert Schweitzer (1875-1965)

From "Indian Thought and Its Development" he writes: "The idea of reincarnation contains a most comforting explanation of reality by means of which Indian thought surmounts difficulties which baffle the thinkers of Europe."

Edgar Allan Poe (1809-1849)

"It is mere idleness to say that I have not lived before —that the soul has no previous existence. You deny it—let us not argue the matter. Convinced myself, I seek not to convince."

Ralph Waldo Emerson (1803-1882)

"The soul is an emanation of the Divinity, a part of the soul of the world, a ray from the source of light. It comes from without into the human body, as into a temporary abode, it goes out of it anew, it wanders in ethereal regions, it returns to visit it. . .it passes into other habitations, for the soul is immortal. . ."

Charles C. Emerson (1808-1836)

The brother of Ralph Waldo states in his "Notes from the Journal of a Scholar" the following: "The reason why Homer is to me like a dewy morning is because I too lived while Troy was, and sailed in the hollow ships of the Grecians to sack the devotee town. . ."

Henry David Thoreau (1817-1862)

"I lived in Judea eighteen hundred years ago, but I never knew that there was such a one as the Christ among my contemporaries. . .and Hawthorne [Nathaniel (1804-1864) American author], too, I remember as one with whom I sauntered in old heroic times...As far back as I can remember I have unconsciously referred to the experiences of a previous state of existence."

Louis May Alcott (1832-1888)

This American author of popular novels for young people writes in a letter to a friend: "I think immortality is the passing of a soul through many lives or experiences, and such as are truly lived, used, and learned, help on to the next. . .I seem to remember former states and feel that in them I have learned some of the lessons that have never since been mine here and in my next step I hope to leave behind many of the trials I have struggled to bear here and to begin to find lightened as I go on. This accounts for the genius and great virtue some show here. They have done well in many phases of this great school..."

Charles Dickens (1812-1870)

Whenever one uses the word "scrooge" as a descriptive adjective, they owe it to this English novelist and his book *A Christmas Carol*—of course he wrote many other books that are familiar to us all. Dickens wrote in his *Pictures From Italy* the following: "At sunset, when I was walking on alone, while the horses rested, I arrived upon a little scene, which, by one of those singular mental operations of which we are all conscious, seemed perfectly familiar to me, and which I see distinctly now. . .In the foreground was a group of silent peasant girls, leaning over the parapet of the little bridge (in Ferrara). . .In the distance a deep dell; the shadow of an approaching night on everything. If I had been murdered there in some former life I could not have seemed to remember the place more thoroughly, or with more emphatic chilling of the blood, and the real remembrance of it acquired in that minute is so strengthened by the imaginary recollection that I hardly think that I could forget it."

Count Leo Tolstoy (1828-1910)

This Russian novelist and philosopher, author of *War and Peace,* writes in his diary: "How well it would be, could one describe the experiences of a man who in a former life committed suicide. He will ever be meeting the same demands that formerly faced him, and so he will arrive at the awareness that he has to fulfill those demands. Set right by this experience, this man will be wiser than others."

These are only a few examples of well-known individuals who

embraced the doctrine of reincarnation. Many poets, such as Henry Wadsworth Longfellow (1807-1882), Oliver Wendell Holmes (1809-1894), Walt Whitman (1819-1892), and Robert Frost (1874-1963) all included references to reincarnation in their works.

It is also the opinion of some researchers that Mark Twain, George Bernard Shaw, and Shakespeare were favorably disposed. Of course, it is well known that Dr. Rudolf Steiner (1861-1925), Austrian philosopher, educator, and founder of Anthroposophy accepted reincarnation as fact as did Goethe (1749-1832).

Many members of the Christian clergy, including Belgian Cardinal Mercier (1851-1926) and Polish Archbishop Passavalli (1820-1897), have also accepted the doctrine.

The following is from Head and Cranston's *Anthology:*

> In the Jewish faith, the *Cabala* is said to represent the hidden wisdom behind the Hebrew scriptures. The first Jews to call themselves "Cabalists" were the Tanaiim who lived in Jerusalem about the beginning of the third century B.C.
>
> In his book *Nishmath Hayem*, the "revered son of Israel" Rabbi Manasseh ben Israel (1604-1657) writes: "The belief or the doctrine of reincarnation of souls is a firm and infallible dogma accepted by the whole assemblage of our church with one accord, so that there is none to be found who would dare deny it. . .Indeed there are a great number of sages in Israel who hold firm to this doctrine so that they made it a dogma, a fundamental point of our religion. We are therefore in duty bound to obey and accept this dogma with acclamation. . .as the truth of it has been incontestably demonstrated by the Zohar and all the books of the Cabalists."

Head and Cranston also quote several passages from the sacred text of Islam, the *Koran,* believed to contain the revelations made by Allah to Mohammed; we find:

> And when this body falleth off all together, as an old fish-shell, his soul doeth well by the releasing, and formeth

a new one instead. . .Ye who now lament to go out of this body wept also when ye were born into it. . .The person of man is only a mask which the soul putteth on for a season; it weareth its proper time and then is cast off, and another is worn in its stead. . .I tell you of a truth, that the spirits which now have affinity shall be kindred together, although they all meet in new persons and names. . .God generates beings, and sends them back over and over again, till they return to Him.

So what happened? Why isn't reincarnation an important doctrine of the Jewish, Christian, and Muslim religions?

With regards to Christianity, most scholars, researchers, and investigators point to the year A.D. 553 as the crucial one. As one German writer states, "May I, for instance, perhaps remind you that the so decisively important doctrine of reincarnation, of rebirth as a human being, through which the Love and Justice of God first became intelligible to us human spirits, was only expunged from Christian creeds by a very small majority decision at the Council of Constantinople in the year 553."

And who were the major players? In this all sources agree and point to the Byzantine Emperor Justinian (483-565) and his Empress, Theodora (508-547). To reduce the large amount of material on this particular subject is difficult, but I will try. As always, you can "look it up!"

Neither of these individuals seems to be of stellar character. One researcher compares Justinian to Adolph Hitler, and describes Theodora as a "tyrant in the grand manner of the more corrupt Caesars." Procopius (500-565), the Byzantine historian, in his book the *Secret History*, is highly critical of Justinian and Theodora and the Byzantine court. According to Head and Cranston: "The Fifth Ecumenical Council of Constantinople is believed by many to have been responsible for the elimination of the doctrine of reincarnation by way of the condemnation of the teachings of Origen concerning the pre-existence of the soul."

Although the Pope, Vigilius, was in Constantinople at the time, he refused to attend. And it is reported that Justinian and Theodora were in complete control of the proceedings and successful in condemning Origenism and, by implication, the doctrine of reincarnation.

Head and Cranston explain that today there has arisen a debate centered around the question "Did the Fifth Ecumenical Council examine the case of Origen and finally [condemn his teachings]?" They conclude that, in light of the evidence we now have, ". . .it would be the height of rashness to give a dogmatic answer to this question. Scholars of the highest repute have taken, and do take today, the opposite sides of the case. . ."

Did the "Church" consequently do away with reincarnation in 553? Dr. MacGregor reports that this was an "assumption" of the Catholic Church that took hold and later was "presupposed" by the Council of Lyons in the thirteenth century and the Council of Florence in the fourteenth; for they insisted "that at death souls go immediately to heaven, hell, or purgatory."

Finally, from Head and Cranston:

> In the light of the references to reincarnation in the Bible, and of statements by the early church fathers, and now the position of Catholic scholars in disclaiming the crusade against Origen, it is not remarkable that a growing number of Christian clergy and religious writers are speaking favorably of the new interest in reincarnation, and are even hoping that this "lost cord of Christianity" may once more vibrate in harmony with Christ's teaching of hope and responsibility.

In a subsequent book written by Head and Cranston, *Reincarnation In World Thought,* it appears that they deemed it appropriate to recognize the obvious reality concerning the belief in—or the denial of—the doctrine of reincarnation. Perhaps the response to their first book was as controversial—"for" and "against"—as the subject itself. For early on, in the Preface of *Reincarnation In World Thought,* they quote British physicist, Raynor Johnson, as follows:

> Some people seem curiously and almost instinctively interested in these topics, others, frequently religious-minded people, feel antagonistic, as though some strange pagan faith were subtly menacing their cherished beliefs. The average thoughtful Western man has in general given

little consideration to these matters. . .In any attempt to formulate a philosophy of life and endeavor to see meaning in our pilgrimage, these ancient beliefs cannot be lightly set aside. It is our duty to weigh them carefully, and without prejudice, in order to see if they will illuminate for us tracts of experience which would otherwise remain dark and mysterious. . .The idea of reincarnation presents no logical difficulties, whatever be the emotional reaction to it. What the soul has done once by the process of incarnation in a physical body, it can presumably do again.

I guess there will always be heated debates over the translation and interpretation of ancient documents and manuscripts. Furthermore, it would probably be next to impossible for an impartial group of open-minded experts to have access to Church archives, the records, and all of the subsequent historic information that has more than likely remained under lock and key or been discarded for one reason or another.

Yet, with so much seeming injustice and inequities in the world, so many questions seem to go unanswered and to tug at the conscious of many. It would be nice to know for sure if reincarnation "was or wasn't" or "is or isn't." I have faith that the truth would eventually surface and thus the debate would finally be put to rest. If the answer is "wasn't or isn't," then at least those concerned could search in some other arena for an understanding of the dilemma that first attracted them to the reincarnation doctrine; and thus their interest in the subject and the pronouncements of psychics like Edgar Cayce.

And finally, as long as I'm off on this tangent, there could be a strong argument that whether we all live a bunch of lives or not doesn't really matter. Today is the first day of the rest of our lives, and what has been, or how we have lived in the past cannot be changed. The only thing that counts is what we do with this life from this moment on.

In 1937 a Cayce reading lectures:

For to find only that you lived [another life], died, and were buried under the cherry tree in grandmother's garden does not make thee one whit a better neighbor, citizen, mother, or father. But to know that ye spoke unkindly [in that past life] and suffered for it, and in the present may correct it by being righteous—that is worthwhile. What is righteousness? Just being kind, just being noble, just being self-sacrificing, just being willing to be the hands for the blind, the feet for the lame—these are constructive experiences. Ye may gain the knowledge of same [past lives]. For incarnations are a fact. How may ye prove it? In thy daily living." (5753-2)

Certainly, as you will possibly conclude as you read on, our everyday decisions and actions might be more positive in nature and our grasp of life more complete if we are aware of the "System," the "Rules," how it works, and the consequences of our actions in the life we lead.

But for you and your brother, Amy, your friends and others, there is still much more awareness that will most likely be new insights on the many theories of the "real world" of the soul.

What If You Had Died Yesterday!

A large number of human beings around the world die every day, and of course a large number are born. Death of the physical body is something that can happen to anyone at any time. At some time in the future we all have to leave our bodies behind and become part of a different world than the one we experience on earth. And although all human being know that there is no way to escape the absolute certainty that their own deaths are only a matter of *when* and not *if,* few have been able to describe with certainty what they expect to encounter once the life-giving force of their physical body ceases to function.

Think about it! Yesterday you were Amy Beth Kay. Then something happened—you're deceased! It's not important how you died, but you've "passed away." The government will soon remove you from their census count. Your Social Security number will be canceled or placed on the inactive list. Food, clothing, and shelter no longer matter. Money and possessions you were sure you needed have lost their significance. Funeral preparations are being made—your casket has been purchased!

Within a few days, your grief-stricken family and friends will be gathered around your closed casket suspended on heavy ropes over a large hole in the ground into which you are about to be lowered and covered with dirt. . ."dust to dust—ashes to ashes. . ."

Where are you? What's the world around you like? Don't say it's too morbid—not now! Why not now? The more you know about "death" the less apprehension as you carry on with your daily life on earth. We see death all around us every day. Yet we are told so little about it.

As Dag Hammerskjold, the late Secretary-General of the United Nations, so aptly expressed: "If we go to the root of the matter, it is our concept of death that decides our answers to all the questions which life poses."

Some people don't believe in an afterlife at all. They seem to think that humans are nothing more than a highly evolved animal that simply ceases to exist at death. Others aren't sure, so they have decided to deny, or at least ignore the question completely—why spend time and energy on such an unpleasant thought when no one knows for sure. They have more important things to do!

There are those who have convictions concerning the subject to a greater or lesser degree who are not members of any religious belief system. And then of course there are those who are members of one of the many organized religious denominations that adhere to the teachings of that religion and therefore believe in the doctrine as put forth in their accepted scriptures and by their leaders.

So much confusion! Can anyone tell us for sure? And with so many different ideas and theories—who can say?

Well, because of the pioneering research done by such persons as Doctors Ramond A. Moody, Jr., Kenneth Ring, Elizabeth Kubler-Ross, and George G. Ritchie, Jr., and other researchers, a fairly clear picture has emerged.

Working with people that were "clinically" dead and then, after a period of time—usually a few minutes to an hour—were "not dead," these researchers have compiled an enormous amount of data on what has become commonly know as the Near Death Experience (NDE).

The stories of all individuals, almost without exception, tell of the same experience as they check out of the Mother Earth Hotel and travel to a new tourist attraction in the sky.

However, before we look at their findings, assumptions and conclusions, one should attempt to decide (or at least keep an open mind) as to whether they believe absolutely, or at least in the possibility, that they have a soul.

Secondly, if we do have a soul, what form does it take when we lay the physical body aside?

And thirdly, what is the make-up or substance of the soul and the world that the soul will experience once it departs the physical body?

All of this, of course, brings us to the much used, and sometimes abused, word or term, *ethereal* [eth-ear-ee-al].

The *American Heritage Dictionary* states that the word *ethereal* is defined as "resembling ether in lightness. . .highly refined. . .delicate. . .of the celestial spheres; heavenly. . ."

Do we have two bodies, the physical one and ethereal one? According to the accounts of NDE-ers, the Edgar Cayce readings, and the pronouncements of every other psychic and metaphysical source I've read, the answer is a definite yes.

If we do, what's it made of—in what form or type of "matter" does it function?

In describing the substance ether, which the dictionary states *ethereal* resembles, we find that in physics the term *ether* means "an all-pervading, infinitely elastic, massless medium formerly postulated as the medium of propagation of electromagnetic waves."

The electromagnetic spectrum is "the entire range of radiation extending in frequency approximately from 10-23 cycles per second to 0 cycles per second (or, in corresponding wave-lengths, from 10-13 centimeter to infinity) and including in order of decreasing frequency, cosmic-ray photons, gamma rays, x rays, ultraviolet radiation, visible light, infrared radiation, microwaves, radio waves, heat, and electric currents." (*American Heritage Dictionary*)

In his book, *The Second Coming,* author Kirk Nelson reports concerning ethereal energy and its relationship to physical matter: "About 50 years ago a Yale University neuroanatomist [one who studies the human nervous system] named Harold Burr found that there are electrical currents within all living organisms from seeds to human beings. He theorized that this electromagnetic field doesn't just reflect the activity of the cells it envelopes; *it also controls and organizes them. "* [My italics.]

So, the conclusion could be drawn that we have an ethereal soul body made up of electrical energy. Furthermore, we could venture that the "waves" it radiates from the physical body might be visible under certain circumstances, or possibly observed by certain human beings. Following this line of thought summons up the term *aura* [or-ah] that is familiar to many.

The first encounter that people have concerning the aura is

usually of the "halo"—a luminous ring or disk of light surrounding the heads or bodies of sacred figures such as saints in religious paintings. These were portrayed in a white or gold-toned white color by the artist. It seems obvious that they knew something of the aura, or why would they have portrayed it—and was there a reason they didn't apply a different color other than white or a gold-toned white?

From what little I know about auras, it suggests that the human body has an electrical "force field" that is completely immersed in every cell of the flesh body and surrounds it extending outwards a few inches. It is not part of the flesh body; it is the spirit part of a *soul body* which gives life to the flesh body with the necessary energy to sustain physical life. Thus the conclusion that a person has passed when the doctor's instruments can no longer register electrical impulses from a person's brain.

Because the soul and physical body are one and the same when visiting planet earth, thoughts, actions, and deeds of a person appear to influence the spectrum field of the person and radiate different colors for a variety of reasons.

Thus the aura that most can't see, but at times can feel or sense as an unexplained energy about another person when in their presence—intuition. "I don't like his/her energy!"

Cayce claimed that he had been able to see auras from a very young age and assumed everyone could. The following story, by columnist Henry Driver, appeared in a local newspaper, *The Ocean View Times*, in April 1989:

> Regarding Edgar Cayce, here is a story that was passed down to me by Langley Land's mother.
>
> "She was standing in her yard, when Mr. Cayce came by to be neighborly; she passed the time of day, as she usually did.
>
> "While Cayce was there, a man went by with a frown on his face. Cayce, turning to Mrs. Land said, 'That man has a terrible aura. In fact, he has an awful burden on his heart. He has committed some horrible crime.'
>
> "'Why Mr. Cayce, what do you mean?' Mrs. Land asked.
>
> "'God has given me a blessing, which at times I feel is almost a curse. That is, that I can see the personality of a

man or woman, which emanates from them in a glow of colors, which is called an aura. That man's was really frightening.'

"Mrs. Land didn't think much of this, but two weeks later, she saw that the *Virginian-Pilot* and the *Princess Anne Free Press* carried front page stories with a picture of the man who had passed in front of her house that day when Edgar Cayce and she were talking. He had been arrested for murder."

So perhaps the golden-white color is the aura a highly evolved spiritual person emanates, at least at certain times, and the other colors are not as spiritually influenced.

Perhaps, just prior to death, the aura seems to disintegrate or depart from the human form, sort of as if the soul of the person "knew" its earth body was about to die.

The following is Edgar Cayce's story about an event that occurred while he was shopping at a department store:

One day, in a large city I entered a department store to do some shopping. I was on the sixth floor and rang for the elevator. While I was waiting for it, I noticed some bright red sweaters and thought I would like to look at them. However, I had signaled for the elevator, and when it came I stepped forward to enter it. It was almost filled with people but suddenly I was repelled. The interior of the car although well lighted seemed dark to me. Something was wrong. Before I could analyze my action I said, "go ahead" to the operator, and stepped back. I went over to look at the sweaters, and then I realized what had made me uneasy. The people in the elevator had no auras. While I was examining the sweaters, which had attracted me by their bright red hues—the color of vigor and energy—the elevator cable snapped, the car fell to the basement, and all the occupants were killed.

This seems to be a good example of some sort of karmic vibrational protection that, because it was not Edgar Cayce's "time," was able to influence his actions. Kind of the way we humans who can't see auras will at times still get a feeling or uneasiness about some situation that may be warning us to think before we leap.

Before returning to the Near Death Experience, let's address another supernatural occurrence that many people claim to have encountered, the Out-of-Body Experience (OBE). There has been ongoing research in the field of parapsychology concerning OBEs for many years.

This type of "happening" almost always takes place when a person is sleeping. The ethereal body is loosened from the physical body and journeys "over there" for a while. Most trance psychics, including Cayce, claim that they leave their bodies when their conscious mind is set aside. This to gather information on the subject of the inquiry. Cayce explained that his ethereal body left by way of the area of the solar plexus of his body when giving a reading, but seemed to remain connected by a sort of life-giving force. Others have reported a similar experience and the term *silver cord* has become a popular description of this sort of electrical cable that bridges the material and ethereal bodies.

There is an interesting reference in the New Testament of the Bible concerning OBEs. The apostle Paul, in Second Corinthians (12:1-5) writes: "I am obliged to boast. It does no good; but I shall go on to tell of visions and revelations granted by the Lord. I know a Christian man who fourteen years ago (whether in the body or out of it, I do not know—God knows) was caught up as far as the third heaven [is there more than one heaven??]. And I know that this same man (whether in the body or out of it, I do not know—God knows) was caught up into paradise, and heard words so secret that human lips may not repeat them. About such a man as that I am ready to boast, but I will not boast on my own account, except of my weakness."

Was Paul referring to himself? Was this a subtle effort by Paul to mask his true identification as this man? Was he hinting about an event that was a personal experience earlier in his life?

Recently, a good friend of mine, whom we will designate Gerald—not his real name—to protect his privacy at his request ("people would think I was weird or a kook"), told me of an experience he is convinced was an OBE. He is not psychic, and nothing like this experience had happened previously, nor have any subsequently.

He was married to his first wife and living with her and their two young sons in Virginia Beach at the time. His father had died the year before. His mother was still living in the same family home in Pittsburgh where he had grown up.

He and his wife were not getting along, and he was seriously thinking about divorce. This for him was a very difficult decision, and he labored and became overwrought concerning his predicament. He worried about the effect a divorce would have on his two sons; he worried what the reaction of his mother would be; and he wished his father were still alive so he could discuss the situation with him, seek his advice, and possibly his approval.

One evening he was especially upset over his dilemma and retired to bed earlier than usual. After lying awake for several hours, he finally entered the sleep state.

The next thing he remembers is floating above his body and looking down at himself in the bed where his physical body was sound asleep. Suddenly he was flying through the air in a western direction at a tremendous speed. Then, what seemed like but a few seconds, he reached his destination—his parent's house in the city of Pittsburgh.

He recognized his mother, but she wasn't aware of his presence. Thereupon, while standing by the fireplace in the living room, his father appeared in a ghost-like form that was easily recognizable.

He distinctly recalls that during this entire adventure, he somehow knew that a bright, luminous strand made up of an array of twisted, beam-like light fibers, was attached to his "travel-body" and at the same time to his physical body in the bedroom in Virginia Beach.

This resembles the similar accounts of many psychics and OBE-ers. In their attempt to portray their interpretation of the ethereal interlude and having concluded upon recall that their experience was genuine, they describe this sort of illimitable electrical umbilical cord, the "silver cord."

Gerald discussed his marital problems with his father at some length and received his father's somewhat reluctant agreement that a divorce was the best decision for all concerned under the circumstances.

Then—but I'll let Gerald tell the rest of the story in his own words: "The next thing I knew I was racing through the sky toward my home in Virginia Beach. I arrived in my bedroom, and very quickly, my body, like a powerful vacuum cleaner, sucked me back into it. I awoke with a start, and was sweating. I was shaking—I'd had the hell scared out of me!"

In her book *Out on a Limb*, author and actress Shirley Mac-Laine, in describing her fascinating OBE experience, writes: "I watched the silver cord attached to my body. . .It glistened in the air. It felt limitless in length. . .totally elastic, always attached to my body. My sight came from some kind of spiritual eye. It wasn't like seeing with real eyes. I soared higher and wondered how far the cord would stretch without snapping. The moment I thought about hesitation, my soaring stopped. I stopped my flight, consciously, in space. As it was, I could see the curvature of the Earth, and darkness on the other side of the globe. The space surrounding my spirit was soothing and gentle and pure."

The Near Death Experience seems to be somewhat different than the Out-of-Body Experience.

Regarding the NDE and the silver cord, I do not know if the cord remains attached to the physical body of the NDE-er or not. There are fascinating theories, opinions and assumptions concerning the silver cord that will be considered in the next chapter. In other words, is the silver cord a necessary contingency in that it acts as a sort of spiritual energy "life-line" and is therefore not completely severed until certain events occur on the other side.

I know you have seen several video tapes about individuals who have "died"—gone to one of the heavens [if Paul is correct in separating or assigning different levels to the "beyond," perhaps as "In my Father's house are many mansions" (John 14: 2)], and returned to tell about their experience. And many people have appeared on radio and T.V. talk shows to tell of their NDEs. Many books are also available on the subject, some by the NDE-ers themselves, and others by researchers and investigators.

Because the NDE-er's physical body has ceased to function, or at the very least is in a comatose state, the road the soul's ethereal body travels once it departs the physical form may be longer than that of the OBE-ers. Depending on the individual, most excursions are different to a lesser or greater degree, each having a diversity and pattern that seems to best suit the stage of that soul's development, and one that is further dependent upon the life lived by the person while on planet earth.

The first step for most on their NDE journey usually finds the ethereal body floating above the physical body and observing the activities of human beings in the immediate vicinity. Many times it is the doctors or emergency personnel attempting to resuscitate the lifeless body.

Next, the decision is made by someone in a professional capacity that the vital signs of the body are no longer functioning, and that the person is "dead."

Many NDE-ers recall being covered with a sheet and left for the attendants from the morgue. One reports he even remembers being wheeled off by the attendants to the "ice box" in the hospital's basement.

One of the truly exceptional video tapes I've seen about NDEs, and perchance the most investigated and documented, is about an ex-Marine named Dannion Brinkley.

He has appeared on many talk shows and has described his experience to audiences throughout the United States and in several other countries including Russia.

The video was filmed at a lecture he gave in Texas in 1993. He told of being electrocuted and pronounced dead. He absented his body, traveled to the beyond, but was then faced with quite a problem when he returned. For, when his ethereal body had once again occupied his physical body, he found himself paralyzed, completely covered with a white sheet, and about to be wheeled into the elevator by the morgue attendants.

He quickly surmised that, because he couldn't move or talk, he was in trouble. Suddenly, in desperation, while flat on his back with the sheet covering his face, he started to sputter and blow air on the sheet over his mouth.

It worked! He was hastily placed on life-support apparatus and started what turned out to be a very long, painful, and tedious recovery.

His chronological account of his unimpaired experience in the beyond is typical of others who report back from the ethereal territory.

Once he was out of his body, Dannion's "awareness" increased. But more importantly to him at the time, he no longer had any physical pain. Soon, he would realize that any speculation, and any fear of death or the unknown, would no longer be puzzling or a complexity.

After leisurely hanging around his badly blistered and seared physical body—riding with it in his ethereal body in the ambulance with the medics as they frantically tried to revive him, he was summoned, but not prepared, for his next great, unforgettable adventure. The same experience that so many others have described when they encounter the "real world" after leaving our human world that is so obviously deficient of the most important ingredient of life—*immortality*.

It was "tunnel time" for Dannion! For somewhat like my friend Gerald, that immense vacuum cleaner in the sky was about to suck his ethereal body, with its *mind* and *free will* intact and undiminished, through the "this side—that side" connecting tunnel and its first whistle-stop, the indescribable light at the other end.

At this point in the chronicle, it is important to note that the descriptive term *tunnel* is about the best most reluctant ethereal pilgrims can utilize in their attempts to explain or describe the first sensation of their journeys.

And more importantly, although most were bewildered and disoriented at suddenly encountering this rather long, dark cylindrical passageway that surrounded them, they, for whatever reason, were not afraid. Why?

Could it be: "Yea, though I walk through the valley of the shadow of death, I will fear no evil; for thou art with me; thy rod and thy staff they comfort me" (from the fourth verse of the 23rd Psalm)? Maybe.

Edgar Cayce said in a reading in response to an individual who was worried about whether his mother had made the transition from this life peacefully and without difficulty:

"Lo! I am with thee, and though I walk through the valley of the shadow of death, my spirit shall guide thee. . .Your mother is alive and happy. Just as is given, the entity may know that all force goes to show, to prove, to bring to the consciousness of the entity, that through that as ye LIVE in Him ye shall be made ALIVE in Him! For there is no death, only the transition from the physical. . ." (136-33)

As the NDE-er steps on the platform at the first way-station, many are greeted by deceased relatives, friends, or helpers. Soon thereafter, they usually find themselves in the exclusive company, "one-on-one," of what is described as a "being of light." They are at once overcome by a presence of powerful, unconditional love. Some claim this being is Jesus; others use the terms "spiritual" or "heavenly" to describe a religious-type entity, such as an angel. One could hazard a guess that a Muslim might be welcomed by Mohammed or one of the prophets of Islam, a Buddhist by the Buddah or a Lama, and so forth. Thus this ethereal light form has an individualized intelligence that is more aware, and seems to be more spiritually mature, than that of the NDE-er. The identification of this Light entity is usually of a personal significance to the arriving soul.

The next step is to be ushered to a front-row-middle seat in the "earth-life review theater." The film about to be projected on the screen is a play-back of every single word, thought, and deed of the NDE-er's soul experience during its sojourn in a physical body while on earth.

Furthermore, the theater is one of tremendous, advanced ethereal technology! For not only does the lone patron see his life story on the screen, but emotions and feelings are also part of the drama that the soul must absorb. And they are more intense than the ones associated with its activity on earth. For if he harmed another, he would not only see and feel the mental and emotional hurt and response of the harmed person; he would also see and feel the mental and emotional reactions of every other individual with whom the harmed party came into contact—a "ripple effect" that one observes when throwing a stone into a pond or other body of still water. So if the NDE-er, say as a husband, was rude or mean to his wife, and she later "took it out" on their child, and the child got in a fight with a friend, and the friend's mother became upset, and on and on, the emotions of the entire expanding scene, from one person to the next, and the next, and the next, would be felt.

On the other hand, if he had shown another love by some generous deed or a kind word of encouragement, he would also experience a much stronger "good feeling" than he had at the time of his action on earth because the energy radiated out from the recipient and affected others.

The total combination of the life review is characterized by those that have participated as a sort of "judgment of the soul"! But according to the witnesses that have had to pass through this seasoning, there is never any sense or personal feeling of condemnation or reckoning from the light being. They say it's much worse! For this exercise is one of forced soul self-examination, excluding nothing, without any opportunity to rationalize or make excuses. And as Dannion and others have exclaimed, the soul is a highly critical and harsh taskmaster when judging itself. It knows what it has done and what has to be done—what detrimental attributes need to be purged—so it can establish a continuing regimen or curriculum for its own positive spiritual development.

Once the painstaking (at least for most) life review experience is thoroughly incorporated into the consciousness of the soul, it usually moves on in the ethereal world and is shown various expressions of the countless forms of activity that are being experienced by other developing souls. Some NDE-ers don't get into this too much before they return; a few seem to get a fairly broad picture of God's Creation. In his recent book *Saved by the Light*, Brinkley details many of his extended adventures before returning to his earth body. He claims to have been shown predictions for the future of our present time, which were recorded in the middle 1970s by NDE researcher Dr. Raymond Moody, of which many have occurred as documented.

At some point in their travels, the NDE-ers claim they are either asked if they want to return to their earth bodies, or they are not given a choice. In the first instance they seem to decide to return to be of assistance to humanity in one way or another. In the second, they understand that they need to complete something that was part of their souls' purposes on earth, and was interrupted. Either way, the fear of death will not be a part of their physical consciousness any more.

One of the most interesting ethereal travelogs of a Near Death Experience that has been related in book form is that of George G. Ritchie, M.D. At the age of 20 he was serving as a private in the Army in Texas. In December 1943 he died of pneumonia. While his body was stretched out on a Army cot in the medical ward covered with a sheet, he found himself engaged in an amazing adventure.

Here we have an example of a NDE-er who is a professional plus the author of a wonderful book, *My Life After Dying*. This book deals with many subjects besides the NDE travelog, but that is our primary concern here. His description of what he was shown on the other side by his special Tour Guide was, for me when I first read it, equivalent to the joining together of a puzzle in a clear, concise, and pictorial form, all of the bits and pieces of everything I had studied. For although the beginnings of his NDE experience was typical, I sense he was, for whatever reason, taken on a special, expanded journey in the ethereal world. A world on the other side that is one of "consequence"—the ethereal destination of each soul that corresponds with the conscious experiences with which it preoccupied itself while inhabiting a human body on planet earth.

I've read books and listened to and watched many video tapes about the destination of the human soul once it departs the body. The Cayce readings speak of planes, spheres, and realms on the other side—where every soul will find an ethereal "parking place" so it can shop in the store of "meeting oneself" for that perfect-fit apparel best suited for the development of its individual, self-conscious soul.

The following excerpts, taken from several chapters of Dr. Ritchie's book, beg serious consideration. We will begin with his account of the events surrounding his physical death.

Since I collapsed in front of the x-ray machine at approximately 3:10 a.m. on December 20, 1943, and remained unconscious until the morning of December 24, 1943, what is recorded here has been related to me by other people.

The doctor in charge of the medical ward to which I was carried was Donald G. Francy, M.D. The nurse assigned to my case was 1st Lieutenant Retta Irvine. . .

That morning my condition continued to deteriorate. When the ward enlisted man made his rounds, he could find no vital signs. He quickly summoned the officer of the day, but this medical officer could detect no evidence of respiration, blood pressure or cardiac impulse. He pronounced me dead, and ordered the attendant to prepare my body for the morgue.

The ward boy had to finish his medication rounds before he could carry out the doctor's orders. Then he came back to the isolation room to which I had been brought. Because I was the same age as he, and because he was having trouble accepting the pronouncement of death on someone as young, the ward boy went back to the officer of the day and told him he thought he had seen my chest move. He asked the medical officer if he wouldn't make up a hypo of adrenaline to have ready to give to me. The medical officer did this and followed the attendant back into my room.

The doctor again checked my vital signs and found none. When the medical officer was about to tell the attendant to go ahead and prep me for the morgue this young attendant asked the doctor to please give me the hypo to be sure. Though the doctor was sure of his diagnosis of death, he could see that this young man was having a hard time dealing with my death. For the ward boy's benefit, he plunged the hypo directly into my heart. To his surprise, my heart started beating. It was four more days and nights before I regained consciousness. The doctor knew for a certainty, it had been 8 to 9 minutes between the two times I had been pronounced dead. I'm sure as an M.D. myself, the doctor must have become very worried, since no one was sure of how long my vital signs had ceased before the ward boy made his rounds. For then, as now, doctors knew the chance of brain damage after five minutes without oxygen to the brain was profound. This is why Dr. Francy made this statement in his notarized statement: "I, speaking for myself, feel sure that his [Dr. Ritchie's] virtual call from death and return to vigorous health has to be explained in terms of other than natural means."

The NDE travelog of Dr. Ritchie takes place during the same "earth time-frame" that Dr. Francy and the ward boy are dealing with his dead physical body. And although Dr. Ritchie may only have been dead for 8 or 9 minutes, as you will later see, time in the beyond—"eternity time"—is not much of a factor as compared to time on this side.

The night was getting stranger and stranger, I thought.

Here I was sitting on the side of my bed; I felt like I just woke up but I did not remember sitting up. What was going on? The last thing I could remember was my standing in front of the x-ray machine. What was I doing in this little room. . .

What time was it? Where was the watch I usually wore on my left arm? I knew it must still be night because it was still dark. . .

I had to leave immediately. . .I walked to the ward hall. . .As I passed through the ward door a ward man, carrying a covered tray, came toward me.

"Watch where you are going," I said. He acted as though he could neither see or hear me. He walked right through me!

This surprised and confused me but I didn't have time to mull it over. . . I passed through the outside door and as soon as I did, to my amazement, I found myself approximately five hundred feet above the ground, traveling at terrific speed. It was a clear night. I was sure, from the position of the North Star, that I was headed in an easterly direction. . .

Quite a bit of distance later, I saw a large river with a big bridge crossing over it. There was a city located on the eastern banks. I came down closer to the ground when I noticed bright blue color from a Pabst Blue Ribbon Beer neon sign in front of a white cafe. . . I saw a tall, thin man, bundled in a dark overcoat coming up the sidewalk, heading toward the door of this cafe. I lit down about twelve feet in front of him to ask directions. I had no idea where I was or how far I had traveled.

"What is the name of this city?" . . .For the second time that night, here was another man who acted as though he could neither see or hear me. In fact he also walked right through me. This was too much.

I went over to lean against the guy wire, the cable coming from the telephone pole and my hand went through it. I suddenly thought, "What has happened to me? No one can see or hear me. . .I have never had to face any problem like this. . .what was that covered mound I left in the bed after I stood up in the room in Texas? Could that have been a body? I don't like this line of thought: A human isn't separated from their body. . .*unless they are dead!*

"If I am, then what is this thing that I am in now? It can go through doors without opening them. It can fly. It does not feel cold. As remarkable as these qualities are, they are no good to me if I can not be seen. I have to go back to that hospital in Camp Barkeley and get my other body!

"I am too young to die. I'm only 20 years old. I have too many things to do with my life. *I have to get back to that hospital.*"

I had no sooner thought about returning to the hospital when I found myself up in the air and traveling, this time rapidly, in a westerly direction. Before I could adequately take in what was happening to me, I found myself standing in front of the Barkeley Station Hospital.

I had made two other discoveries about this strange out-of-body realm. First, one goes wherever his/her soul's sincere desire leads him/her. Secondly, time in this realm, if it exists at all, is much shorter than our normal human realm, or the capacity to cover great distances in a regular period of time is vastly increased, for the distance I knew I had traveled could not have been covered in our fastest airplanes.

I was in trouble now, for when I left the hospital, I was in such a great rush that I had not taken the trouble to look and see which ward I had left. . .I continued to search from ward to ward and room to room. I had begun to believe I was going to be condemned to spending an eternity doing this when I came to a poorly lit room. It only had a night light on in the stalk of the lamp.

Lying in the bed with a sheet pulled up over the head was this body. . .the left arm and hand uncovered. There on the left ring finger was my Phi Gamma Delta and University of Richmond ring. . .I did not like the color of the hand because it had the same appearance my grandfather's hand had three years before when I saw it right after he died. Now my massive denial was breaking down and I was going to have to accept the fact that I was dead. . .I have never felt so alone, discouraged and frightened. *"Oh God, where are you when I am so lost and discouraged?"*

I could walk through the bed and walls. I could not pick up the sheet when I wanted to pull back the covers to look at the face to make sure it was my body. . .I had discovered it was impossible to get the spiritual or soul body into or through any of the small openings in the human body. I was fini, caput, at my end, and giving up.

Suddenly an amazing thing began. The light at the end of the bed began to grow brighter and brighter. . .It continued to increase in intensity until it seemed to be equal to a million welder's lights. I knew if I had been seeing through my human eyes instead of those of my spiritual body I would have been blinded.

Then three things happened instantaneously. *Something deep inside of my spiritual being said: "STAND UP. YOU ARE IN THE PRESENCE OF THE SON OF GOD."*

I was suddenly propelled up and off the bed. Out of the brilliant light at the end of the bed stepped the most magnificent Being I have ever known.

The hospital walls disappeared and in the place of them was a living panorama of my entire life where I saw in detail everything I had ever experienced, from my own caesarean birth through my present death. . .

Dr. Ritchie, after his brief life review, was now ready to accompany Jesus on a tour of the various spheres, planes, or, as he names them—"realms."

The First Realm: Earth

Since the first realm is earth, the place where I had spent 20 years of my life, it would take many books to record everything the panorama recorded. I have only touched upon enough incidents to drive home some points. . .It has taken me forty-five years since the experience to develop a vocabulary that can begin to express the ideas I hope to get across.

I want the reader to realize that as the Christ and I observed these beings of Earth and the other three realms of this planet, these beings could not see us. They not only could not see us but the beings from one realm could not perceive the beings from another realm. I was made aware of but one realm at a time.

I have placed the name, the name I felt would be easiest to understand, on the different realms. The world religions and the denominations within a religion have often used different names for the same realms, which has made the task of understanding the realms more difficult for the layman. As an example, I hear my Catholic and Mormon brothers and sisters describing the same realm by entirely different names. . .

Now for my experiences in the first realm:

I was standing in front of this majestic Being. . .This was no sweet gentle Jesus, meek, weak or mild. Here stood a robust male who radiated strength. . .

Here stood a Being that knew everything I had ever done in my life, for the panorama of my life surrounded us, and yet He totally accepted and loved me. I have never felt such love and compassion. Before He entered the room, I was desperately alone and frightened and could only think about how I could return to my body so I might be able to continue my life on earth. After being in His presence and feeling His love, I never wanted to leave Him again for any reason. Nothing I had, no one I had ever known on earth could make me want to leave Someone who loved and accepted me like this One.

When He spoke, I heard Him in a way different from anyone else. I heard Him from deep within in my own mind. My mind, not my brain, for my human brain, as far as I could understand, was in my head and body lying on the bed, and it still looked just as dead as when I had first come back into the room. . .

He notified me mentally that He wished me to stay close to Him. We left the hospital room by rising straight up through the roof and then we headed over the surface of the Earth at a very rapid speed.

We came over an extremely large city beside a great body of water. As we descended into the heart of the city, I felt that my spiritual eyes must be out of focus. I could see the human beings and the material world, but I could also see other beings without physical bodies. They were dispersed amongst the human beings, who also had an electrical field around them.

Suddenly the Christ and I lit on the street outside this tavern and immediately went in, to observe what was happening. From this point to our return to the hospital room, the Christ said nothing but was taking me to different places to observe, learn and form my own conclusions.

I could see the civilians and service personnel having a good time drinking their beer, wine, and highballs in the booths and at the bar. I could see other beings who were experiencing the same difficulty I had had when they went to pick up a drink. Their hands went right through the glasses the same way that mine had gone through the guy wire of the telephone pole. Then they would stand and watch in great anguish. From time to time one of the human beings would become totally intoxicated, which caused the electrical field or aura to separate, starting at the head and going to the feet. When this would happen, one of the less dense beings without the aura would try to beat out the other similar beings getting into the human being through the separated electrical field. ["Possession: controlled by a spirit force"?]

To save words, I shall call this realm and the beings who belonged to this realm *astral*. Though the Lord did not make any explanation, I gathered that these astral beings had become alcoholics when they were living on the earth and had never been able to rid themselves of their addiction while they were human beings. They were still driven by this addiction and the only way they apparently could enjoy feeling intoxicated again was to enter a human's aura. This would profoundly affect my professional life, causing me to spend much time working with alcoholics and other substance-abuse cases.

If only the people who are now calling for the legalization of these extremely addicting drugs could have seen what I saw, they would realize they need to have a better understanding of what happens to us after we pass through death. Human beings become addicted here and if they don't overcome the addiction while they are still alive, the Lord was showing me that this addiction does not stop just because they die.

In fact, this was what Jesus had tried to teach us by repeating the great commandments. We have to be careful of what we grow to love so much that we let it control us, for it can lead us into becoming bound on this Earth to the things that we made false gods.

We changed our location and moved to a large plant in the industrial section of this city. The year was 1943. Because of the war effort, most of our larger manufacturing plants were on three shifts, which worked around the clock. I could see humans on the assembly lines and the foreman and other officers. I could also see astral beings standing beside each of them trying to tell them how to do their jobs, but the human beings could neither hear nor see them, just as the ward attendants could not see me.

This time we moved to the suburbs of the city and I could see a young man walking down the sidewalk. Beside him was this being walking, trying to tell him how to dress and what to do with his life but he could neither see nor hear her. I gathered she had been his mother when she was human.

The Second Realm: Astral, Purgatory? Terrestrial?

I do not know how to adequately explain what is happening but it appeared we were going deeper and deeper into the astral realm, into an area where it no longer overshadowed our material realm. The astral realm has its own reality of substance to it as does our earthly realm with all our buildings and things man has constructed. When we first came down into the city I could see the physical city that any of us would see if we were landing at night by a jet airliner. What made me feel as though my vision was out of focus was seeing another city superimposed on our physical city. I came to realize this [astral city] belonged to these astral beings. In the deepest sense most of the beings of one realm weren't aware of the existence of the other. When I say we were going much deeper, I mean we were becoming so much a part of the astral dimension that we could no longer see the physical beings or our physical material physical structures.

We were still in the same area where the large city had been visible but all I could see now was the dwelling places where astral beings lived which were definitely of a less dense material or more ethereal and I had the impression they were more a product of their thoughts than humans in our realm.

Just as there are areas in our cities which are divided by ethnic and moral standards so it is, in the astral realm. There were definite areas of this dimensions that I would not want to be caught in, just as there are areas in our own towns and cities that we don't feel safe in.

There were two other things distinctly unique about the beings of this realm. Since hypocrisy is impossible because others know your thoughts the minute you think them, they tend to group with the ones who think the same way they do. In our own plane of existence, earth, we have the saying "Birds of a feather flock together." The main reason that they stick together is because it is too threatening to be with beings with whom you disagree when they know it.

It also seemed that the longer beings were in any of these realms, the closer they came in appearance to being around 30 to 35 years of age.

One of the places we observed deep within this realm seemed to be a receiving station. Beings would arrive here oftentimes in a deep hypnotic sleep. I call it hypnotic because I realized they had put themselves in this state by their beliefs. This was during the middle of World War II and I saw many young beings arrive here as a result of their physical death. Here were what I would call angels working with them trying to arouse them and help them realize God is truly a God of the living and that they did not have to lie around sleeping until Gabriel or someone came along blowing on a horn. . .

The Third Realm: Hell

We were in another place where people arrive who had committed suicide out of hatred, jealousy, resentment, bitterness and total disdain for themselves and others. I want to make clear that it was impressed upon me that these were the ones who had the same type of powerful emotions which people who committed murder have. The only difference is they believed because of their religious teaching that committing murder was a worse sin. Their motivation was: "If I can't kill you, I shall kill myself to get even with you."

I am not talking about people who are what we call insane and no longer responsible for their action. Nor am I speaking of people who are dying from a horrible long-suffering illness. . .

I understood from what I was seeing that these people and the average murderer also are confined in a state where they are given a chance to realize two very important facts. One, you can kill the physical body, not the soul. Two, that only love, not hate, can bring themselves and others true happiness. I believe once they fully understand this, they are given the opportunity to continue their spiritual and mental growth.

We were in another location of this plane. We were standing on a high porch in front of this huge building. What I saw horrified me more than anything I have ever seen in life. Since you could tell what beings in this place thought, you knew they were filled with hate, deceit, lies, self-righteousness bordering on megalomania, and lewd sexual aggressiveness that were causing them to carry out all kind of abominable acts on each other.

This was breaking the heart of the Son of God standing beside me. Even here were angels trying to get them to change their thoughts. Since they could not admit there were beings greater than themselves, they could not see or hear them. There was no fire and brimstone here; no boxed-in canyons, but something a thousand times worse from my point of view. Here was a place totally devoid of love. This was HELL.

There were beings arguing over some religious or political point, trying to kill the ones who did not agree with them. I thought when I saw this, "No wonder our world is in such a mess and we have had so many tragic religious wars. No wonder this was breaking Christ's heart, the One who came to teach us peace and love." Yes, this place was absent of any other beings, except the angels, who understood what Jesus had incarnated to try to teach us.

The Fourth Realm: Realm of Knowledge, Paradise? Terrestrial?

It is beyond my capacity to explain how the Lord closed one realm and opened another. It was not a matter of us changing location as much as it was a case of the location changing right in front of our vision. If the previous realm evoked horror and irreparable despair, this realm gives hope, joy, and a challenge to keep learning in all fields of knowledge which help us and our fellow human beings.

It is the realm which removes forever the concept that we stop learning or progressing in knowledge when we die. I could call this realm the realm of research, or the mental realm or the realm of intellectual, scientific and religious knowledge. All would be correct.

This is the realm where I believe the souls go who have developed the greatest interest in a particular field of life's endeavor, the ones who want to keep on researching and learning more in their particular field. . .

It seemed to me that this dimension is divided into centers of higher learning. The only things on earth that begin to approach these centers are our most advanced universities and large industrial research centers. . .

In each one of these research laboratories, the beings inside were using instruments I had never seen and could not begin to understand. . .

I felt they were far more advanced than most of the beings I had seen on earth in the arts and sciences. I understood that their work was motivated by sincere interest in what they were learning and a desire to help make the universe a better place to live, not money or fame. They were so far advanced in so many ways that it would be like taking my son, when he was six years of age, to one of the research laboratories at the University of Virginia and expecting him to comprehend what he was seeing. . .

Again we were moving to a new area of study, and lit in front of the largest library I had ever seen. It was bigger than all the buildings in downtown Washington, D.C., put together. It housed the holy books of the universe. One could place all the holy books of this earth in just one room of this library.

The beings here were dressed in brown monkish robes. They were as intent on their studies of the numerous volumes as had been the beings in the other centers of learning that we had visited.

Noticing the color of the dress of these beings made me aware of something. There were no racial color differences, I suddenly realized, in any of the realms which I had been shown.

I became aware that the Christ was watching these souls in their study of the universe's religions and saw he did not judge any of them. They too were not judging the religions which they were studying but were interested in the many different ways the beings of the universe had attempted to come to understand their Creator. I suddenly realized how wrong it was for any of us on earth to judge another's approach to God or to feel we have the only answers. . .

The Fifth Realm: The Celestial Realm, or Heaven

Again he instructed me to move close to His side and we started traveling through space at an incredible speed. This is the first time we had left this planet. We were now approaching an amazing place, realm, planet or what shall I call it? The only thing I heard when I was growing up which pictured such a place was the song my stepmother used to sing called "The Holy City." In it was described the new Jerusalem. This must have been it, for the light which shown upon its street was brilliant.

We never actually reached the streets or open places, for while we were only a short distance above the surface, two of these beings who could see us as well as we could see them started towards us.

Now this was surprising because this was the first realm in which the inhabitants could see the Christ and myself. Even more amazing, they exuded light almost as brilliant as the Christ. As the two beings approached us, I could also feel the love flowing from them toward us. The complete joy they showed at seeing the Christ was unmistakable.

Seeing these beings and feeling the joy, peace and happiness which swelled up from them made me feel that here was the place of all places, the top realm of all realms. The beings who inhabited it were full of love. This, I was and am convinced, is heaven. As marvelous as I thought the previous realm was, after glimpsing this new realm we were seeing, I began to understand for the first time what Paul was saying in the 13th Chapter of First Corinthians when he wrote: "If I have the gift of prophecy and can fathom all mysteries and all knowledge, and I have a faith that can remove mountains, but have not love, I am nothing." I do not infer that the wonderful souls on the fourth realm did not have love because they did, but not to the degree that the souls of this realm had reached.

I, of course, wanted to go in to be with these beings but the Christ was already beginning to move us further and further away from them. He was taking me back toward earth. . .

In what seemed a very short time but an extremely long distance, we were back in front of the hospital at Camp Barkeley. He then led me directly into my hospital room and did a startling thing.

He opened a corridor through time which showed me increasing natural disasters coming upon this earth. There were more and more hurricanes and floods occurring over different areas of our planet. The earthquakes and volcanoes were increasing. We were becoming more and more selfish and self-righteous. Families were splitting, governments were breaking apart because people were thinking only of themselves. I saw armies marching on the United States from the south and explosions over the entire world that were of a magnitude beyond my capacity to imagine. I realized if they continued, human life as we have known it could not continue to exist.

Suddenly this corridor was closed off and a second corridor started to open through time. At the beginning they appeared very similar but the further the second one unfolded, the more different it became. The planet grew more peaceful. Man and nature both were better. Man was not as critical of himself or others. He was not as destructive of nature and he was beginning to understand what love is. Then we stood at a place in time where we were more like the beings in the fourth realm. The Lord sent a mental message to me, "It is left to man which direction he shall choose. *I came to this planet to show you through the life I led how to love. Without OUR FATHER you can do nothing, neither could I. I showed you this. You have 45 years.* "

He then gave me orders to return to the human plane and mentally said, "You have 45 years. . ."

The next thing I remember was looking down at my left hand and seeing my Phi Gamma Delta ring on my second finger. Again I passed into unconsciousness and remained in it until the morning [on Christmas eve, more than four days later] I opened my human eyes.

One of the experiences related by Dr. Ritchie seems to confirm the statements in an unusual Cayce reading. While at the tavern with Jesus, Dr. Ritchie describes what is known as "possession" [maybe the same phenomenon as the accounts in the Bible of Jesus commanding evil spirits to leave a person]. Intoxicated, the human "electrical field or aura [would] separate starting at the head and going to the feet. When this would happen one of the less dense beings. . .without the aura would try to beat out the other similar beings getting into the human being through the separated electrical field."

In 1938 a lady with an alcoholic husband requested a reading about his problem. The following excerpts are from the question-and-answer section of the reading:

Q: What causes my husband to lose control of himself?
A: Possession!
Q: What is meant by possession?
A: Means POSSESSION!
Q: Is he crazy or mentally deranged?
A: If possession isn't crazy, what is it?
Q: Does possession mean by other entities, while under the influence of liquor?

A: By other entities [departed souls] while under the influence of liquor. For this body (the husband), if there could be a sufficient period of refraining from the use of alcoholic stimulants and the diathermy electrical treatments used, such treatments would drive these entities out! But do not use electrical treatments with the effects of alcohol in the system, it would be detrimental. (1183-3)

I'm not familiar with the term "electrical diathermy treatment," but I assume that by applying its electrical energy to this man's body it would somehow repair his "blown open" aura by increasing the vibration and thus seal it, so as to prevent entrance from the addicted ethereal boozers on the other side! I wonder what it's like for ethereal drug addicts and what control they have over their counterparts on the earth?

I wonder what breed of depraved and evil spirits are attracted to people who fool around with satanic rituals and paraphernalia. Do these entities affect them while awake, or even more so when their protective energy body is loosened from the physical body while sleeping—as it does with stimulants. It's something to think about!

Dr. Ritchie's final experience before returning to his physical body, the natural disasters and so forth, will be covered in a later chapter.

Was Dr. Ritchie really "dead"—completely and totally? Or was that mysterious silver cord still attached to his physical body?

The Mystery of the Silver Cord

I've not come across a lot of material on the silver cord, but what has been brought to my attention has motivated me to speculate or theorize about it. Is there any connection (no pun intended) between this unsubstantiated ethereal "something" or "spirit transmission line" and the reports in the New Testament of the Bible of the miracles of Jesus in raising people from the dead? Does the silver cord scenario have anything to do with the reports that both Peter and Paul did the same?

At the occasion of what is known as the Pentecost, observed by members of various Christian denominations seven weeks after Easter, it is reported in the New Testament in the second chapter of the Acts of the Apostles:

> . . .they [the Apostles and followers of Jesus] were all together in one place, when suddenly there came from the sky a noise like that of a strong driving wind, which filled the whole house where they were sitting. And there appeared to them tongues like flames of fire, dispersed among them and resting on each one. And they were all filled with the Holy Spirit and began to talk in other tongues, as the Spirit gave them power of utterance.
>
> Now there were living in Jerusalem devout Jews drawn from every nation under heaven; and at this sound the crowd gathered, all bewildered because each one heard his own language spoken. They were amazed and in their astonishment exclaimed, "Why, they are all Galileans, are they not, these men who are speaking? How is it then that we hear them, each of us in his own language? Parthians, Medes, Elamites; inhabitants of Mesopotamia, of Judaea and Cappadocia, of Pontus and Asia, of Phrygia and Pamphylia, of Egypt and the

districts of Libya and Arabs, we hear them telling in our own tongues the great things God has done." And they were all amazed and perplexed, saying to one another, "What can this mean?" Others said contemptuously, "They have been drinking!"

The Apostle Peter was in charge at the time. Did he (and perhaps others), because of this visit from God's Spirit, acquire certain supernatural capabilities?

And, from a later event, what about Saul before he changed his name to Paul, the Greek equivalent. Was he "zapped" by the Holy Spirit too?

From the 9th Chapter of The Acts of the Apostles we are told:

Meanwhile Saul was still breathing murderous threats against the disciples of the new way of the Lord. He went to the High Priest and applied for letters to the synagogues at Damascus authorizing him to arrest anyone he found, men or women, who followed the new way, and bring them to Jerusalem. While he was still on the road and nearing Damascus, suddenly a light flashed from the sky all around him. He fell to the ground and heard a voice saying, "Saul, Saul, why do you persecute me?" "Tell me, Lord," he said, "Who you are." The voice answered, "I am Jesus, whom you are persecuting. But get up and go into the city, and you will be told what you have to do." Meanwhile, the men who were traveling with him stood speechless; they heard the voice but could see no one. Saul got up from the ground, but when he opened his eyes he could not see; so they led him by the hand and brought him into Damascus. He was blind for three days, and took no food or drink.

There was a disciple in Damascus named Ananias. He had a vision in which he heard the voice of the Lord: "Ananias!" "Here I am Lord," he answered. The Lord said to him, "Go at once to Straight Street, to the house of Judas, and ask for the man from Tarsus named Saul. You will find him in prayer; he has had a vision of a man named Ananias coming in and laying his hands on him to restore his sight." Ananias answered, "Lord, I have often heard about this man and all the harm he has done to thy people in Jerusalem.

And he is here with authority from the chief priests to arrest all who invoke thy name." But the Lord said to him, "You must go, for this man is my chosen instrument to bring my name before the nations and their kings, and before the people of Israel. I myself will show him all that he must go through for my name's sake."

So Ananias went. He entered the house, laid his hands on him, and said, "Saul, my brother, the Lord Jesus, who appeared to you on your way here, has sent me to you so that you may recover your sight, and be filled with the Holy Spirit." And immediately it seemed that scales fell from his eyes, and he regained his sight.

It is obvious from the many accounts of His miracles in the Bible that Jesus utilized the power of the Holy Spirit. He could also do a lot of zapping while still on this side.

Three of His most impressive miracles had to do with His ability to "raise the dead." And in addition to the miracles preformed by Jesus, it is also interesting to ponder the reported miracles preformed by the Apostles Peter and Paul. They too must have had a little of the zap in them after they were visited by the Holy Spirit.

Starting with Peter in the Acts of the Apostles (9:36-43), we read:

> In Joppa was a disciple named Tabitha (in Greek, Dorcas, meaning a gazelle), who filled her days with acts of kindness and charity. At that time she fell ill and died; and they washed her body and laid it in a room upstairs. As Lydda was near Joppa, the disciples, who had heard Peter was there, sent two men to him with the urgent request, "Please come over to us without delay." Peter thereupon went off with them. When he arrived they took him upstairs to the room, where all the widows came and stood round him in tears, showing him the shirts and coats that Dorcas used to make while she was with them. Peter sent them all outside, and knelt down and prayed. Then, turning toward the body, he said, "Get up, Tabitha." She opened her eyes, saw Peter, and sat up. He gave her his hand and helped her to her feet. Then he called the members of the congregation

and the widows and showed her to them alive. The news spread all over Joppa, and many came to believe in the Lord. Peter stayed on in Joppa for some time with one Simon, a tanner.

In Chapter 20:7-12, we find:

On the Saturday night, in our assembly for the breaking of bread, Paul, who was to leave the next day, addressed them, and went on speaking until midnight. Now there were many lamps in the upper room where we were assembled; and a youth named Eutychus, who was sitting on the window-ledge, grew more and more sleepy as Paul went on talking. At last he was completely overcome by sleep, fell from the third storey to the ground, and was picked up for dead. Paul went down, threw himself upon him, seizing him in his arms, and said to them. "Stop this commotion; there is still life in him." He then went upstairs, broke bread and ate, and after much conversation, which lasted until dawn, he departed. And they took the boy away alive and were immensely comforted.

Next, in the order they appear in the New Testament, are the three accounts about Jesus:

Even as He [Jesus] spoke, there came a president of the synagogue, who bowed low before Him and said, "My daughter has just died; but come and lay your hand on her, and she will live." Jesus rose and went with him, and so did his disciples.

Then a woman who had suffered from hemorrhages for twelve years came up from behind, and touched the edge of his cloak; for she said to herself, "If I can only touch His cloak, I shall be cured." But Jesus turned and saw her, and said, "Take heart, my daughter, your faith has cured you." And from that moment on she recovered.

When Jesus arrived at the president's house and saw the flute-players and the general commotion, He said, "Be off! The girl is not dead; she is asleep"; and they only laughed at him. But, when everyone had turned out, He went into the room and took the girl by the hand, and she got up. This story became the talk of all the country round. [Matthew 9:18-26.]

. . .Jesus went to a town called Nain, accompanied by His disciples and a large crowd. As He approached the gate of the town He met a funeral. The dead man was the only son of his widowed mother; and many of the townspeople were with her. When the Lord saw her his heart went out to her, and He said. "Weep no more." With that he stepped forward and laid His hand on the bier; and the bearers halted. Then He spoke, "Young man, rise up!" The dead man sat up and began to speak; and Jesus gave him back to his mother. Deep awe fell upon them all, and they praised God. "A great prophet has arisen among us," they said, and again, "God has shown His care for His people." The story of what he had done ran through all parts of Judaea and the whole neighborhood. [Luke 7:11-17.]

There was a man named Lazarus who had fallen ill. His home was at Bethany, the village of Mary and her sister Martha. . .The sisters sent a message to Him: "Sir, you should know that your friend lies ill." When Jesus heard this He said, "This illness will not end in death; it has come for the glory of God, to bring glory to the Son of God." And therefore, though he loved Martha and her sister and Lazarus, after hearing of his illness Jesus waited for two days in the place where He was.

After this He said to His disciples, "Let us go back to Judaea.". . .On His arrival Jesus found that Lazarus had already been four days in the tomb. Bethany was just under two miles from Jerusalem, and many of the people had come from the city to Martha and Mary to condole with them on their brother's death. As soon as she heard that Jesus was on His way, Martha went to meet Him, while Mary stayed at home.

Martha said to Jesus, "If you had been here, Sir, my brother would not have died. Even now I know that whatever you ask of God, God will grant you." Jesus said, "Your brother will rise again."

. . .So Mary went to the place where Jesus was. As soon

as she caught sight of Him she fell at His feet and said, "O Sir, if you had only been here my brother would not have died." When Jesus saw her weeping and the Jews and her companions weeping, He sighed heavily and was deeply moved. "Where have you laid him?" He asked. They replied, "Come and see, Sir." Jesus wept. The Jews said, "How dearly He must have loved him!" But some of them said, "Could not this man who opened the blind man's eyes, have done something to keep Lazarus from dying?"

Jesus again sighed deeply; then He went over to the tomb. It was a cave, with a stone placed against it. Jesus said, "Take away the stone." Martha, the dead man's sister, said to Him, "Sir, by now there will be a stench; he has been there four days." Jesus said, "Did I not tell you that if you have faith you will see the glory of God?" So they removed the stone.

Then Jesus said, "Father, I thank thee; thou hast heard me. I knew already that thou always hearest me, but I spoke for the sake of the people standing round, that they might believe thou didst send me."

Then He raised His voice in a great cry: "Lazarus, come forth." The dead man came out, his hands and feet swathed in linen bands, his face wrapped in cloth. Jesus said, "Loose him; let him go." [John 11:1-44]

I know you're aware of the three volumes consisting of 168 "essays" entitled *In the Light of Truth;* also known as the "Grail Message." So I thought this might be a good time to introduce this individual who lived in Austria and Germany about the same time as Cayce, was teaching and prophesying, and appears to have had clairvoyant ability. Certainly, much of his information mirrored Cayce's, but not all. Like most material of this type, there are differences, and I can't accept a number of conclusions or some of the claims that are expressed in his writings. As usual with material of this type, I attempt to compare and relate it to all other information of the same classification. I do feel he had the capability to "see" the events and happenings in much of the ethereal world, the ability to observe many of the previously described realms. How far his clairvoyance permitted him to penetrate different realms, the maximum "altitude" of his clairvoyant reach, I do not know. And just as important, along with his visions was the necessity of "interpretation" and the ability to translate his experiences into words.

Many have found the explanations in his essays concerning Creation and what he designates Divine Laws very perceptive. His name was Oscar Ernst Bernhardt. His writings were authored under the pen name Abd-Ru-Shin. His essays have been translated from the German into several languages.

In his essays he at times was stern, inflexible, and foreboding. Of course, considering the times and the environment in which he lived, with Adolph Hitler rising to power, and World War ll looming on the horizon, it is understandable that many of his pronouncements and warnings would be harsh. But then, so were some of the Cayce readings; and the Bible doesn't always read like a romance novel.

Today his lectures or essays and other books and booklets based on his work are published and distributed in about a dozen countries. They cover a lot of territory encompassing the essential questions about life.

Bernhardt was born in Germany in 1875. His literary activity began while still a young man, and he made numerous journeys to distant countries. In 1915 he was interned in England. He was released in 1919, and in 1924 began to write the first lectures of the "Grail Message." Arrested in 1938 by the Nazis, he and his family were placed under house arrest, where he was under the constant supervision of the Gestapo. Prevented from further fulfillment of his task, he died on the 6th of December, 1941. His supporters claim, "His living knowledge is no earthly learnedness; he draws it from purest and highest Sources."

One of the booklets that is based on the "Grail Message" is taken from a lecture that was presented in Germany about fifteen years ago by Dr. Richard Steinpach. The title is a long one: *How Is It That We Live After Death And What Is The Meaning Of Life.* There are explanations and conclusions in this booklet that deal with the silver cord. So here are the excerpts that I feel need to be a part of our "awareness experience" as we proceed with ethereal matters:

And now. . .let us turn to death. When, in the opinion of science, does it take place? The view held today is that brain-death is the decisive sign. By that it is understood the cession of the brain-current on the electro-encephalograph. This is in complete agreement with what sleep-research has established, and at the same time with what we have heard about the magnetic union of body and soul brought about by radiation. . .the cessation of this wave-pattern appears to medical science to be death. But what is the brain-current, other than a measurable vibration peculiar to the body? And vibration in its turn is only a manifestation of radiation, because all radiation appears as vibration, is vibration. If such a vibration is no longer present as measurable, this to the doctor signifies death. Thus you see that science strictly establishes what matters, but it sees only the fact and does not yet recognize its actual significance.

But as can already be ascertained during the gradual attainment of sleep, the decline in the body-radiation does not take place suddenly. If we disregard those cases in which the body is destroyed by violence or mutilation, then it is a question of a smooth, gliding process, as if one were slowly and steadily reducing the current of an electro-magnet and finally switching it off. This explains the difficulty in accurately determining the time of death. It was formerly thought that it had set in when respiration ceases, thereafter, when the heart stops. Now it is assumed that a person is dead when the brain-current stops. But where actually is the end? How is it possible for the "clinically dead" to be able to come back to life?

I would like to tell you this in words from the "Grail Mesasage". . . "Upon its exit and departure the soul draws the astral [dense ethereal] body with it out of the physical body. That is how it appears. In reality the soul only pulls it off the physical body, because there was never a fusion but only a sliding into one another, as with a collapsible telescope. In doing so, the soul does not draw this astral body very far, because it is anchored not only with the soul but also with the physical body; and moreover the soul, from which the actual movement issues, wants to sever itself also from the astral body, and accordingly strives away from it as well. Thus after the earthly departure of the soul the astral always remains near the physical body. The further the soul moves away, the weaker the astral body also becomes; and the ever-advancing severance of the soul finally brings about the decay and disintegration of the astral body, which in turn immediately brings in its turn the decay of the physical body, in the same way it also influenced its formation.. .."

This brings to mind the "astral city" superimposed on top of the "physical city" that Dr. Ritchie described—but it was apparently of a different astral consistency than the astral substance that forms the human body—thus perhaps, the "as above—so below" saying; what is below, what takes form or occurs in physical matter is first somehow formed in one of the astral realms of the ethereal world.

It further brings to mind a similar description in a Cayce reading.

In 1935, a lady who had been having out-of-body experiences and was "seeing things" asked Cayce:

Q: In regard to my projection of myself into the astral plane, about two weeks ago; some of the people were animated, and some seemed like waxen images of themselves. What made the difference?

A: Some—those who appear as images—are expressions or shells; or the body of an individual which has been left when its soul-self has projected onward, and the astral body has not yet been dissolved—as it were. . .

For what individuals are, lives on and takes form in what is called by others the astral body. The soul leaves this behind it and it appears as seen (waxen). Other individuals, as in your experience are in their animated form because it is their own [realm] of experience at the present time. (516-4)

Dr. Steinpach continues:

For the severance of the soul does not always take place so simply. I may remind you that not only is the soul kept within its denser coverings through the mutual radiation [electromagnetic energy], but it has in the already mentioned "silver cord" a direct lead, a connection to the astral body, and thereby the physical body. . .in the limited continuation of this connection-cord also lies the explanation of how it was by the persons interviewed by the thanatologists, several of whom had indeed been considered "clinically dead," could return to life. In all these cases the connection-cord simply was not yet severed.

This natural fact also explains the alleged miracle of the waking of the dead, thus also that of Lazarus. In this Creation nothing can take place that would not be in accordance with its Laws. To return to life is always only possible for him whose "line" between spirit and earthly body still exists, thus making re-entry possible. The miraculous in such happenings lies in the to us incomprehensible power which brings about such a return. In the cases reported by Dr. Moody [*Life After Life*], it was of an other-worldly nature; in the case of Lazarus through Jesus, even of a Divine kind.

Especially from the Biblical accounts of the raising of the dead by Jesus can the increasing distance of the soul from the body be recognized, and the ever greater force that is needed in order to strengthen the radiation-connection again.

In the case of the daughter of Jarius, who had just departed this life, Jesus (according to Luke 8, 54) simply says: "Maid arise"; with the young man of Nain, who is about to be buried, He already becomes more urgent: "Young man, I say unto thee, arise" (Luke 7,14); finally in the case of Lazarus, who had already been lying in the grave for four days, Jesus prays, before crying with a loud voice: "Lazarus, come forth." (John 11, 41-43)

And now, after hearing all this, it will be easy for us to understand the experiences of the persons questioned by Dr. Moody. Since to begin with we have also dealt with the subject of sleep, we can undertake to classify the experiences. For they are always to be found in the realm between sleep and death. There are accounts of people who lay seriously ill, and who on the threshold between life and death saw deceased relatives or helpers from the beyond, and spoke with them. Then finally there are those who found themselves already outside their bodies, and of whom some had already been considered "clinically dead." But none of these was really dead, that is the connection-cord had not yet been severed. It is just through this that these descriptions, as intermediate stages on the way from life to death, complement the picture of that smooth transition of which I have already spoken. . .

Dr. Steinpach discusses the tunnel experience of NDE-ers as follows:

. . .this next stage that the soul now enters is actually a world of faster vibration emphasized by an acoustic experience which the persons questioned had while being "pulled out." For they heard a noise, and described it as a booming of a bell, a rushing, a roaring, a bang.

Thereafter they found themselves suddenly in brightness of the new world, the earthly had disappeared from them. Now we know from many earthly phenomena that where two movements of different speed collide, such acoustic effects result. Just think of the uncorking of a champagne bottle, the crack of a whip, or clearer still—the boom that arises when a supersonic aircraft breaks the sound barrier. Thus for the soul, the entry into its new form of existence is like the breaking of a sound barrier. It changes over into a world of faster vibration.

A result of this faster vibration is also a change in the concept of time. One of those questioned by Dr. Moody summarized the experience in the beyond. . ."As soon as one has detached oneself from the earthly body, everything seems to speed up." This too is really self-evident and simply could not be otherwise. For owing to its faster intrinsic movement the ethereal soul-body is lighter, thus more permeable, and that brings with it an increased receptivity to experiencing. For everything that happens affects the spirit much more directly through less dense covering. It is a position to be able at the same time to grasp, that is to experience, much more than we [still in physical bodies] can, because every happening can move the spirit much more directly. Here it is fundamentally a question of the same Law, which indeed we can also observe in the earthly: the more vibrations produced by the current with which we charge a cable, the more conversations we can simultaneously transmit along it. . .the higher the frequency of the light with which we take a photograph, the more detail it will show us. The laser-beam is the clearest example of this. In this increased ability to comprehend, which is characteristic of any faster movement, is found an easily verifiable explanation, based on the Laws of Nature, of the apparently so enigmatic saying "a thousand years are as one day."

But the altered feeling of time in the world beyond shows us very clearly that with regard to the concept of time we are under a misapprehension. We generally understand it by minutes, hours, days, and years. Yet these are basically only a measure, derived from the movement of the earth in relation to the sun. We all know indeed that one hour does not equal another, that an hour of joy seems short to us, while one of pain seems like an eternity. . . Time is not the hour or the date, but the abundance of what we able to experience, to accumulate in it.

Regarding the concept of time, I will again quote from Kirk Nelson's *The Second Coming:*

When one has a grasp of Einstein's theory of relativity: "As an object approaches the speed of light, time slows down; when said object reaches the speed of light, time stops." This part of Einstein's theory was proven in 1936 by Bell Laboratories. . . [so] if a man left earth in a spaceship traveling at the speed of light [186,000 miles per second] when he reached his destination he would be the same age as when he left. Even if several years had passed for people on earth, our space traveler would not have aged at all. All energy moves about the universe at the speed of light. So to energy and light, time is totally meaningless. Einstein put it as follows: "For us believing physicists time has the value of mere illusion, however tenacious." Our brain acts as a brake to slow our consciousness down enough that it can operate at a level where the *illusion of time* does exist, in the physical universe. [Italics are mine.]

I recently spoke with Dr. Ritchie and asked him if he recalled being attached to the silver cord during his ethereal travelog. He answered with a definite "No!" He explained that he and Dr. Moody had discussed this scenario at some length, and had arrived at the conclusion that Dr. Ritchie had indeed died.

I've concluded that, regardless, Dr. Ritchie's case is unique and special—that because of his own soul development he was permitted to do the things he did and see the things he saw. His soul somehow could handle the accelerated energy of an extreme ethereal vibrational altitude.

He also told me that Dr. Moody claimed only a small percentage of NDE-ers he had questioned were aware of being attached on the other side to the silver cord.

Does it matter? Perhaps as it relates to our awareness exercise that assists in some way to expand one's insight. There are differences of opinion in this, as in almost everything. Certainly when dealing with extrasensory, psychic, or clairvoyant information, there are many differences which I will attempt to explain later. There are many influences that need to be taken into consideration. As to authenticity, I am prejudiced in favor of the Cayce readings because of the research and apparent results.

Let me give you an example. Dr. Steinpach, in his lecture based on the "Grail Message," puts forth the following opinion concerning the resurrection of Jesus Christ:

> A positively dramatic account of the existence of such an ethereal body is to be found in the New Testament, according to which after His burial Jesus appeared to Mary Magdalene, and also several times to His disciples. He walked beside them, they spoke with Him, but they did not recognize Him. He entered rooms whose doors were locked—and only when he broke bread with them at the table did they perceive that it was Jesus. This surely testifies quite clearly that He came to them in a different, changed bodily form, in precisely that ethereal body, which they, shaken by the deep experiences of the previous days, were enabled to see at that time. Had it been otherwise, they would surely have recognized Him immediately. But Jesus wished by this not only to tell them that He was risen; He wished to

demonstrate to them that life goes on. . .immediately after earthly death.

Here we have an interpretation put forth in the "Grail Message," by a clairvoyant, of his perception and conclusions concerning the ressurection of Jesus, as explained by an obviously intelligent, informed supporter, Dr. Steinpach.

But let's see what Cayce had to say about the ressurection of Jesus.

On the morning that Christians celebrate as Easter, it is stated in the New Testament that Jesus first appeared to Mary Magdalen, but that she did not recognize Him. Next He warns her, "Don't touch me, for I have not yet ascended to the Father. . .but go to my brothers and tell them that I am now ascending to my Father. . ." It also appears that His disciples did not recognize Him, at least at first, and that He "vanished from their sight" and that on one occasion they were "startled and terrified and thought they were seeing a ghost." What does all this mean?

Did Jesus only appear in His "ethereal" body as Dr. Steinpach claims? Was he able to influence those He chose to see it? Was His pure white, perfect vibration of such a high energy (electrical) that it was "too hot to handle" until He reduced the voltage?

I'm not the only one who has puzzled over all this. Fortunately, in 1944, shortly before Cayce's death, an individual asked him while in a trance: "Is the transmutation of human flesh to flesh divine the real mystery of the crucifixion and resurrection? Please explain this mystery. [From the *American Heritage Dictionary*: *Transmute*: "to transform from one form, nature, or substance into another.] Cayce answered:

> . . .having attained in the physical consciousness the at-onement with the Father-Mother-God, the completeness was such that with the disintegration of the body—as indicated in the manner in which the shroud, the robe, the napkin lay, there was then the taking of the body-physical form. This was the manner. It was not transmutation, as of changing from one form to another.
>
> Having as indicated in the manner in which the body-physical entered the upper room with the doors closed (John

20:26), not by being a part of the wood through which the body passed but by forming from the ether [ethereal] waves that were within the room, because of a meeting prepared by faith. . .

As indicated in the spoken word to Mary in the garden, "touch me not, for I have not yet ascended to my Father." The body (flesh) that formed, that seen by the normal or carnal eye of Mary, was such that it could not be handled until there had been the conscious union with the sources of all power, of all force.

But afterward—when there had been the first, second, third, fourth and even *sixth* meeting—He *then* said: [to the Apostle Thomas, the "doubter"]: "Put forth thy hand and touch the nail prints in my hands, in my feet. Thrust thy hand into my side and believe." This indicated the transformation.

For as indicated when the soul departs from the body (this is not being spoken of the Christ, you see), it has all of the form of the body from which it passed—yet it is not visible to the carnal [earthly] mind, unless that mind has been, and is, attuned to the infinite. Then it appears in the infinite [the other side, or beyond] as that which may be handled, with all the attributes of the physical being; with the appetites, until these have been accorded to a unit of activity [realm] with Universal consciousness.

Just as it was with the Christ-body: "Children, have ye anything here to eat?" This indicated to the disciples and the apostles present that this was not transmutation but a regeneration, recreation of the atoms and cells of body that might, through desire, masticate material things [partake of food]—fish and honey in the honeycomb were given.

As also indicated later, when He stood by the sea and the disciples and apostles who saw Him from the distance could not, in the early morning light, discern—but when He spoke, the voice made the impression upon the mind of the beloved disciple [John] such that he spoke, "It is the Lord!"

Not transmutation of flesh but creation, in the pattern indicated.

Just as when there are those various realms about the solar system in which each entity may find itself when absent from the body, it takes on those other realms not an earthly form, but a pattern—conforming to the same dimensional elements of that individual planet or space [planets = dimensional = realms]." (2533-8)

From (900-227) we find:

Then, as the body of Christ in the flesh became perfect in the world, as it was laid aside on the Cross and in the tomb, the *physical body* moved away—through what man comes to know as dimensions—and the *Spirit* was then able to take hold on that Being in the way in which it entered again into the body. Thus it presented itself to the world, as it did to individuals at the time. . .

In another reading is the following:

. . .He became the first of those who overcame death in the body [and this] enabled Him to illuminate, to so revivify that body [impart new life] that He could take it up again, even when those fluids of the body had been drained away by the nail holes in His hands and the spear piercing His side. . . (1152-1)

Finally, to cut the silver cord completely from the body of this chapter, let's take a look at some extraordinary research about persons who purchased one-way out-of-the-body airline tickets to the ethereal beyond.

To explore the territory of their experiences, we will briefly excerpt passages from another book.

Again, this is a book that I would urge everyone to read to further exploring the views and information expressed in this brief compilation. This is another "look it up" recommendation I hope you act on.

The title is *Life Between Life,* and it was written by a Canadian psychiatrist, Joel L. Whitton, M.D., Ph.D., with Joe Fisher. In the introduction of this book, Dr. Whitton acknowledges that reincarnation is part of his religious tradition. He further states: "Two thirds of Americans believe in life after death. A 1982 Gallup poll showed that twenty-three percent of Americans believe in reincarnation, but only five percent of my psychiatric colleagues do."

Prior to writing this book with Dr. Whitton, Joe Fisher had authored the popular book *The Case For Reincarnation*, which in time was published in more than thirty countries.

Life Between Life came about as the result of a kind of hypnotic, past-life regression accident. Dr. Whitton had been putting his patients into a hypnotic trance for many years. This in an attempt to discover an event in a patient's past life that may have carried over in the memory of the patient's subconscious mind in the present life and was causing some sort of physical, mental, or emotional discomfort.

In this case history which had its beginning in October 1973, he had been regressing a forty-two-year-old woman named Paula. The following account is taken from the book:

> Over the next year she spent more than one hundred hours in deep trance giving coherent descriptions of a long succession of incarnations, most of them female. They included:
>
> • Martha Paine, born on a farm in Maryland in 1822. She died from a fall on the farmhouse stairs while a young girl.
>
> • Margaret Campbell, a housekeeper who lived near Quebec City. She was seventeen years of age in 1707 and later married a fur trapper named Arsenault.
>
> • Sister Augusta Cecilia—age thirty-four in 1241—who spent most of her life working in a Portuguese orphanage near the Spanish border.
>
> • Thelma, the young sister of a tribal leader in Mongolia under Genghis Khan, whom she knew as "Temujin." She described her age as sixteen "summers" at the time she was killed in battle.
>
> Paula's inventory of lives had been traced back to an existence as a slave girl in ancient Egypt when, unpredictably, her hypnotic traveling suddenly changed course. One Tuesday evening in April 1974, as she was talking in a deep trance about Martha Paine's life, Dr. Whitton remembered there were further details he wished to learn about the last days of Margaret Campbell. First he interrupted his garrulous subject. Then he told her: "Go to the life before you were Martha. . ."

Expecting Martha's childlike voice to be exchanged for that of the elderly Canadian housekeeper, Dr. Whitton waited several minutes for the familiar French-accented enunciation. But no sound, save the occasional sigh, came from Paula's mouth. Her lips moved only with a constantly shifting facial expression which indicated she was watching events unfold. But what events where these? Not knowing where she was in time, Dr. Whitton was wondering where he had erred when Paula interrupted his bewilderment with a rapid flickering of her eyelids. Her lips, too, puckered repeatedly as if she were searching for words and not finding them. Then, slowly and with great difficulty, she announced in a dreamy monotone:

"I'm in the sky. . .I can see a farmhouse and a barn. . .It's early. . .early morning. The sun. . .is low and making, making. . . making long shadows across the burnt fields. . .stubbly fields."

Dr. Whitton could barely believe what he was hearing. Paula wasn't supposed to be "in the sky." So he must have made a technical error. . .but which one? Hypnotic subjects have much in common with computer programs in that their wondrous responses rest upon the most literal commands. They must be told exactly what to do. Make one mistake and the show won't go on—at least, not the show anticipated by the hypnotist.

Dr. Whitton had told Paula. . ."Go to the life before you were Martha." Clearly there was a difference between the two [not a specific suggestion as "go to life of Martha Paine"].

"What are you doing up in the air?" asked the puzzled hypnotist.

"I'm. . .waiting. . .to. . . be. . .born. I'm watching, watching what my mother does."

"Where is your mother?"

"She's. . .out at the pump and she's having great difficulty. . .difficulty filling the bucket. . ."

"Why is she having difficulty?"

"Because my body is weighing her down. . .I want. . .I want to tell her to take care. For her sake and for mine. . ."

"What is your name?"

"I. . .have. . .no. . .name."

By committing the mistake of verbal imprecision, he had accidently intruded upon an uncharted realm of human experience—the gap between incarnations.

Thus, this unintentional hypnotic incident began Dr. Whitton's exploration into ". . .What happens to us between earthly incarnations?" By the time this book was published, he had "escorted more than thirty subjects—most of them over a period of several years—into the timeless, spaceless, zone. . ."

The book goes on to summarize certain of the subject's experiences:

> But it wasn't long before their experiences—which ranged from perceptions of a "judgment board" to the writing of "karmic scripts" for the next life [occurred]. . .they realized that they themselves, while discarnate, had actively chosen the setting and involvements of their earthly existence. Parents, careers, relationships, and major events contributing to joys and sorrows were seen to have been selected in advance.

The "judgment board"—what does that mean? The NDE-ers, when reporting back for duty, exclaim that their soul was doing the judging. Is the between lives travelog different than the ones, for example, of Dannion Brinkley? Of course, I don't know, I can only speculate.

In the "mystery of the silver cord," is it possible that the cord remains attached in the case of the NDE experience because they are not yet "dead-dead"? Thus the term "Near Death Experience." Is there still a spark of physical life in the body of the NDE-er that hasn't been extinguished because the silver cord is somehow keeping the glow alive? This even though the vital signs have stopped functioning? To again quote from *Life After Life*:

> The awakening to disembodied existence is where the life between life really begins. Those who have reported "near-death" phenomena such as the overwhelming brilliance of a blinding light and a panoramic review of the life just passed, have been granted a "peek around the corner"

into the interlife. On resuscitation, the subjects of near-death experiences often speak of having approached a border or barrier which they perceive as the frontier between life and death. Dr. Whitton's subjects encounter no such restricting influence on their journeys into the next world because the transition has been completed.

From what I can derive from this book and others, the judgment experience is somewhat different when comparing the NDE-ers with that of the "dead-deaders." But the emotions felt during the judgment experience seem to be pretty much the same. We've seen an example of the judgment experience of an NDE-er while sitting in the life-review theater, and the experience of Dr. Ritchie. But the between-lives life-review theater appears to include an additional dimension—what some refer to as the "spiritual hierarchy" encounter of the soul.

There are many examples in ancient traditions and various mythologies that express the existence of a group of ethereal authority souls that sit in judgment soon after the human soul adjusts itself to its new ethereal surroundings subsequent to its most recent earth life.

To continue with *Life Between* Life:

> The testimony of Dr. Witton's subjects thoroughly endorses the existence of a board of judgment and enlarges considerably on the rather sparse descriptions handed down from the old world. Nearly all [of his subjects] found themselves appearing before a group of wise, elderly beings—usually three in number, occasionally four, and in rare instances as many as seven. . .
>
> The members of this etheric board are highly advanced spiritually and may even have completed their cycle of earthly incarnations. Knowing intuitively everything there is to be known about the person who stands before them, their role is to assist that individual in evaluating the life that has just passed and, eventually, to make recommendations concerning the next incarnation.
>
> If there is a private hell in the life between life, it is the moment when the soul presents itself for review. This is when remorse, guilt, and self-recrimination for failings in

the last incarnation are vented with a visceral intensity that produces anguish and bitter tears. . .While incarnate, one's negative actions can be rationalized and repressed; there are always plenty of excuses available. In the interlife the emotions generated by these actions emerge raw and irreconcilable. Any emotional suffering that was inflicted on others is felt as keenly as if it were inflicted on oneself. But perhaps most distressing of all is the realization that the time for changing attitudes and rectifying mistakes is well and truly past. The door of the last life is locked and bolted and the consequences of actions and evasions must be faced in the ultimate showdown which calls to account precisely who we are and what we stand for.

The author then goes on to describe the many experiences of Dr. Witton's subjects. Many of the accounts are fascinating and an interesting voyage into an altered awareness.

Having now had a peek into the ethereal world of the beyond and the many explanations of the soul's judgment over there, the natural order of things would be to move on and return to our physical world.

As I'm sure you have figured out by now, the combination of a myriad of soul activities through eons of time penetrates or seems to filter down in some form, configuration, or pattern of ethereal substance, and infiltrates the personal earth travelog of each individual in a manner that it affects our daily lives in many ways, both positive and negative.

The Lords of Karma—Or—The Grace of God?

During the past 25 or 30 years I've heard mention of the *Lords of Karma*, what some designate as "task-masters," from time to time. As you previously read in the excerpts from *Life Between Life,* if Dr. Whitton's subjects are accurate in the descriptions of their experiences between lives, maybe there is something to the scenario that the soul is assisted by these members of an ethereal spiritual hierarchy in planning their next incarnation.

So to reiterate, now that we are more knowledgeable about what some say the soul goes through on the other side, it's time to re-enter earth's atmosphere for a little more knowledge concerning our earth life.

It is very unusual for any human being to go through physical life without encountering difficulties. Almost everyone will experience suffering at one time or another. The severity, of course, can vary a great deal with each individual. On the other hand, there are usually many pleasant experiences also. The overall journey of most people being one of a mixed bag. Joy and sorrow taking turns! And let's not forget boredom that many want to avoid.

At least some of this mixed bag of life's events is said to be about the soul meeting itself for the purpose of learning and understanding. When we say a person is lucky, or unlucky, we are using a term to describe what, to the person making this observation, has no obvious explanation. It's as though the luck factor in a person's life, good or bad, is nothing more than an accident. And although the terms "good karma" and "bad karma" are very popular for those that have made reincarnation a part of their philosophy, if the lords of karma were teaching the class, they would attempt to convince the students that all events are for the soul's development.

There are many different types of karma. Each is well explored and explained in many books on the subject. Trying to categorize the various "action-reaction" themes that take place in our lives is almost impossible. However, I have seen this attempted with some success in two excellent books, among other, based on the Edgar Cayce readings. The Cayce readings are loaded with thousands of examples that address karmic situations.

One of the books that researched the readings for the purpose of categorizing the karmic circumstances that people encounter was published in the late 1960s under the title *Many Mansions.* It was authored by psychologist Gina Cerminara, Ph.D. Another was *Edgar Cayce's Story of Karma,* by Mary Ann Woodward, published in the early 1970s.

Most of the cases you are about to read are from these two books. Actually, I'm using a few of the excerpts from readings that are also cited in these two books in order to present the material in a somewhat logical way.

The applicable readings are the chiefly quoted material here, for they pretty much speak for themselves. Since almost everyone is interested in relationships, we will try a few on the subject of *relationship karma*:

> For the home is the nearest pattern in the earth (where there is unity of purpose in the companionship) to man's relationship with his Maker. For it is ever-creative in purpose, from the personalities and individualities coordinated in a cause. (3577-1)

> No entity enters a material sojourn by chance, but from those realms [that term again] of consciousness in which it has dwelt between earthy sojourns, the entity chooses that environ through which it may make manifest those corrections, or those choices it has made and does make in its real or in its inner self. (3027-2)

A husband asked Cayce: "How was I associated with my wife in Palestine?" He answered:

> She was then the entity's daughter. Doesn't she try to boss him now? As the associations come as has been given, the entity has chosen well. We will find much help, mentally, materially, spiritually. (1003-2)

Another fellow asked: "Give past associations with my sister, explain the urges that may be helpful to each other in the present." Answer:

The associations were as brother and sister [in colonial Virginia]. . .They lose patience one with the other just as they did then. These are to be turned, of course, into channels in which there will be "give and take." No one individual knows it all, though each of you feels you do at times. (2460-1)

A young lady with a relationship problem asks: "What was my relationship in the past incarnation with Robert?" Answer:

In the English experience [she had been told of a life in England earlier in the reading]—very unsatisfactory —because he left thee and ye never lost sight of the manner in which ye were treated. And doubts have arisen. Yet there are those obligations, those things that need to be worked out.

Then: "What attitude should I hold for our mutual development?" Answer:

As ye would be forgiven, forgive. (2791-1)

A woman asks: "Why have I always felt one apart from my family—my brother and sisters?" Answer:

Because ye were once cast out by some of those. (2624-1)

A young man inquires: "From which side of my family do I inherit the most?" Answer:

You inherit most from your self, not from family. The family is only a river through which it [the soul entity] flows. (1233-1)

A young bachelor had a list of the names of four girls with whom he was acquainted. He was dating two of them. "With which of these would marriage be successful?" he asked. The answer was fairly typical of the many other questions along the same line:

> This should be determined by the entity itself, in the studying, analyzing, of purposes and ideals. For in the consideration of marriage, if it is to be a success, it must be considered not from merely the outward appearance, a physical attraction; for these soon fade. Rather it should be considered from the angle of spiritual ideals, mental aspirations, and physical agreements. These should be analyzed in the experience of the entity, as in the experience of the companion, in the choice of such relationships. For these relationships are representative of the purpose of propagation of species, as well as those ideals that arise from spiritual and mental relationships. (1776-2)

A lady who was having problems with her marriage asked: "Have I ever contacted my husband in any other life experience; if so, in what way?" Answer:

> He bought you! Doesn't he act like it at times? [She later remarked "He sure does!"] (1222-1)

Well, I think you get the gist of some of the relationship problems that may have had their seeds planted in the past.

The next category is broadly called *physical karma*. Again, the readings are mostly self-explanatory in addressing and discussing the *dis-ease* that most experience to some degree in their lives.

There are many other reasons people become ill besides the ones caused by some karmic influence. Attitude and emotions seem to have a lot to do with these: "To be sure the attitudes oft influence the physical conditions of the body. No one can hate his neighbor and not have stomach or liver trouble. One cannot be jealous and allow anger of same and not have upset digestion or heart disorder." (4021-1)

In dealing with illness, physical deformity, mental retardation, and other malfunctions of the physical body, a reading in tracing at least part of the problem to a previous life stated: "These [karmic] sources of course may be rejected by many. Yet those who reject this do not supply better reasons, do they?" (3504-1)

One such case that was attributed to a previous life was that of an eleven-year-old boy who suffered from enuresis (bed-wetting):

> Before this then the entity was in the land of the present nativity. . .as one Marshall Whittaker. The entity was the minister, or the associate minister, who caused the uprising and the condemnation of children who saw, who heard, who experienced the voices of those in the inter-between. And because of the entity's condemning there was brought a hardship into the experience [in] the adopting of that rule of "ducking" others. Hence the entity physically has experienced the ducking, from its own self, in its daily activities which will grow to become more and more of a hindrance to self, unless there will be set aright that incoordination between the mental mind, or the physical mind and spiritual mind of the individual entity, as related to condemnation of things in others.(2779-1)

The reading advised that the mother give to the boy as he was falling asleep suggestions such as: "You are good and kind. You are going to make many people happy. You are going to help everyone with whom you come in contact." This sort of subconscious therapy eventually solved the problem. Also, the boy's disposition improved according to his mother.

A fifty-three-year-old woman who had suffered a serious back deformity since childhood and had struggled most of her life just to stay alive, was told: "This entity was among those with that one [Nero] who persecuted the church so thoroughly and fiddled while Rome burned. That's the reason this entity in body has been disfigured by structural conditions." Cayce then went on to make an unusual statement that is seldom found in the readings: "Yet may this entity be set apart. For through its experiences in the earth, it has advanced from a low degree to that which may not even necessitate a reincarnation in the earth. Not that it has reached perfection but there are realms for instruction if the entity will hold to that ideal of those [the early Christians who were persecuted in the coliseum in Rome] whom it once scoffed at because of the pleasure materially brought in the associations [she was partying with the wrong crowd] who did the persecuting." (5366-1)

An accident victim, a young man of seventeen who had been paraplegic for two years, also had his situation tied to a life at the time of Nero. His life reading told him that he was to learn patience this time around. He had advanced spiritually in his most recent past life during the American Revolution.

In the present there is that characteristic of orderliness, of cheerfulness; and there are the abilities to make the best of bad situations, the abilities to use that in hand. And would that every soul would learn that lesson, even as well as this entity has gained in the present. It was during those periods when there were the persecutions of those who followed in the way of the Nazarene.

The entity was then a Roman soldier, and one given rather to that of self-indulgence—and glorified rather in seeing the sufferings of those who held to that principle [the teachings of Jesus].

And the entity fought in the arena and watched many that had met the entity [in some sort of combat in the arena] fight again with the beasts [lions]. . .the entity saw suffering, and the entity made light of same.

Hence the entity sees suffering in self in the present, and must again make light of same—but for a different purpose, for a different desire, for a different cause.

For again the entity meets self in that wished, that desired on the part of those against whom the entity held grudges. (1215-4)

In this last reading, I'm guessing that the young accident victim, as a Roman soldier, had to enter into some sort of combat with one or more persecuted Christians. He must have been defeated in some of the contests, for it appears from the reading, that he was a "poor loser" even though the reward his opponents accepted for winning and thus surviving was to be, at some later time, thrown to the lions. He must have held a grudge against them until the final horrors of their lives, and scoffed, or enjoyed their plight in a revengeful way.

From the New Testament Book of Romans (12:19-21) is advice by Paul in a letter to the newly-converted Christians our Roman soldier may have wished he had followed: "My dear friends, do not seek revenge, but leave a place for divine retribution [karma?]; for there is a text which reads, 'Justice is mine says the Lord, I will repay.' But there is another text: 'If your enemy is hungry, feed him; if he is thirsty, give him a drink;'. . .Do not let evil conquer you, but use good to defeat evil."

In another reading a blind man was told: "Before that we find the entity in the Arabian or Persian land. . .There we find the entity came as a dweller from among the Persian peoples; given to what would be termed activities of a barbaric nature. For the entity brought persecution to those of other tribes or other beliefs, by the blinding with hot irons." (1861-2)

These readings are very small examples of the many times unexplained adverse fate enters the lives of individuals. And the variables of the causes and effects are as multitudinous as the human population census.

The readings also have many examples of how that which we think or maybe previously thought we wanted to make us happy, has just the opposite effect. The readings claimed on several occasions that having a lot of money turned out to be a burden instead of a blessing. As one of my friends who seemed to have plenty of money but not necessarily happiness told me: "There are two ways to be a millionaire; one is to increase your income, the other is to decrease your desires!" Without doubt, fame and "position" also had its drawbacks. You can pretty much kiss privacy good-bye if that is the fate you attract.

It's interesting to consider the reactions we have as we experience the different episodes of our life. When something good comes our way, we accept it with a knowing comfort that somehow it is deserved—perhaps a reward for some past deed that escapes us. But when something bad takes place, we have the natural tendency to blame everyone but ourselves, maybe even God, for our unpleasant circumstances.

We all have heard of people who exhibit remarkable talents at a very early age. The child genius who can play the piano with little formal instruction. The math whiz-kid who can deal with complicated formulas far in advance of his or her age group.

People who are natural athletes, sales persons, musicians, etc. The list is endless, but the explanations of the experts hardly have a beginning. But once you study and examine past-life chapters of the autobiographies of individuals, the likenesses of their portraits take shape as the pieces of the puzzle are fitted in place.

The Cayce readings often referred to a sort of *talent karma* when advising people on career paths. But then, a past-life talent may not always fit into contemporary times. We still have to make a living, and sometimes a past-life talent brought over is relegated to that of a hobby.

Quite a few present-life apprehensions and phobias are also represented in the Cayce readings and other literature.

In addition, idiosyncrasies, unexplained fears, and what some label as "abnormalities" are sometimes accounted for when no previous episode of the present life solves the riddle.

At this juncture, rather than excerpt and quote from the Cayce readings and other literature, I will cite a few examples of past-life/present-life circumstances from my memory since they are rather elementary and easy to understand.

I recall the story of a man who lived in England and had been an alcoholic from a young age. He had gone to a great deal of trouble trying to rid himself of his addiction. He saw many professionals and tried various therapies.

In desperation, he agreed to be hypnotized and regressed back to past lives. It turned out that, in his life just prior to the present one, he had been a confederate soldier during the American Civil War. He had been badly wounded and was carried on a stretcher to a medical facility where he was placed on the floor of a large, gymnasium-like building. Many other wounded soldiers were also there including some from the Union Army.

There were no bandages. Medicines of any kind including pain killers weren't available; so the medical personnel were relegated to administering small amounts of strong whiskey every few hours to help alleviate the agony. This went on for several days, and he, like many of the other wounded, were desperate in their anticipation of each dosage.

Then the supply of whiskey became exhausted, and there was no more to be had! He lay there for several more days and finally died—still craving the whiskey. When he entered this time the subconscious craving was still with him.

I recall that the uncovering of this episode seemed to help him understand his addiction and he eventually brought it under control, although I don't recall if he totally quit.

In another example, I remember that a woman asked Cayce why she was afraid of sharp instruments such as knives and scissors. He extracted from her subconscious the details of an event in ancient Persia. A member of an invading horde had taken her life with a sword.

Finally, I recall the problem of a man who suffered from claustrophobia. He could not stand to be closed in and would climb the steps in a high-rise building rather than take the elevator. As a foot soldier in France during the First World War, he had been buried alive in one of the trenches, and suffocated.

After exploring only a few of what must be an endless number of possibilities and explanations of the Law of Cause and Effect—reciprocal action—it may occur to some that the cycles of consequences resulting from past-life events could go on indefinitely. Sort of like placing millions of different colored marbles in a gigantic, empty paint can; placing the can in the universe's herculean shaker that is attached to an endless energy source, and throwing the switch.

The marbles would just keep bouncing off of each other. Each one either striking another, or being struck by another. Each time a marble would whack another, it would mean that the karmic result of their action had been set in motion. In some way it would have to be whacked. The "action-reaction" chain of events would never end—the ultimate dilemma of being caught between a marble and a hard place! And trying to get out of this dilemma, trying to escape—to pry the paint can open from the inside—would seem unlikely.

But, as far-fetched as it may seem to some, there is a way to pry open the can, which envelopes us like the atmosphere of planet earth, and blast off in a space ship to that energy force known as *Grace*.

According to the belief of many, it is because Jesus willingly accepted the crucifixion and completely made His will one with God's will, that humanity is saved by Grace.

To quote one Cayce researcher:

The promise comes from the New Covenant which Jesus proclaimed—that as we live through Him, we live under the Law of Grace rather than the Law of Karma [the previous ones were based on the Mosaic Covenant which embodied the Ten Commandments and the system of religious law built on them that placed moral obligations above political and economic interests. The New Covenant did not replace the moral duties of the previous ones, but was an addition to them].

As we interpret the Cayce readings, the Law of Grace was always a potential for Mankind [the Grace of God] but it wasn't until Jesus accepted the crucifixion and rose from the dead that this New Covenant became a reality for everyone. Yet in reality, the Law of Grace still exists only as a promise to those who willingly follow His last admonition—"That we love one another as He loved us." Otherwise we are still living under the Law of Karma.

In one reading, Cayce tells a 48-year-old woman, ". . .Then as the entity sets itself to do or to accomplish that which is of a creative influence or force, it comes under the interpretation of the law between karma and grace. No longer is the entity then under the law of cause and effect—or karma, but rather in grace it may go on to a higher calling as set in Him." (2800-2)

And in another he states, "Then, in such [wrong] choices, that which has been of the karmic nature becomes the activative principle in the experience. But if there is the [right] choice. . .then the karmic force is not necessarily something that you must meet irrespective. For the way is opened through Him. This ye may accept, this ye may reject." (2487-2)

The "karmic force"! Well by now we should have a pretty good idea of how it influences our lives? But can we comprehend the method applied by the "grace force" to defeat it?

I think it will help in our understanding to return to that "ethereal energy" or "vibration" and enlist the help of the "Grail Message" and its explanation of the method used to acquire Grace.

Men speak of deserved and undeserved fate, of reward and punishment, retribution and karma.

All these are only part-designations of a Law resting in Creation: *The Law of Reciprocal Action.*

A Law which lies in the entire Creation from its earliest beginning, which has been inseparably interwoven with the great, never-ceasing evolution as an essential part of creating itself, and of development. Like a gigantic system of the finest nerve-strands, it supports and animates the mighty Universe, and promotes continual movement, an eternal giving and taking!

Plainly and simply, and yet so aptly, Jesus Christ has already expressed it: *"What a man sows that he shall reap!"*

These few words render the picture of the activity and life in the entire Creation so excellently that it can hardly be expressed differently. The meaning of the words is inflexibly interwoven with life. Immovable, inviolable, incorruptible in its continual operation.

You can see it if you *want* to see it. Begin by observing the surroundings now visible to you. What you call Laws of Nature are, of course, the Divine Laws, are the Creator's Will. You will quickly recognize how unswerving they are in constant activity; for if you sow wheat you will not reap rye, and if you scatter rye it cannot bring you rice.

This is so obvious to every man that he simply never reflects on the actual process. Therefore he does not become at all conscious of the strict and great Law resting in it. And yet he faces the answer to a riddle, which need be no riddle to him.

Now the same Law you are able to observe here takes effect with equal certainty and force also in the ethereal part of the whole Creation, which is by far the larger part. It lies immutably in *every* happening, also in the most delicate development of your thoughts, which also still have a certain element of material substance.

In all existence, visible and invisible to you, it is no different, but each kind produces its own kind. . .The process runs *uniformly* through everything, it makes no distinction, leaves no gap, it does not stop at some other part of Creation, but carries the effects through like an unbreakable thread, without interruption or cessation.

Even though the greater part of mankind, in their limitation and conceit, have isolated themselves from the Universe, the Divine or Natural Laws have not ceased on that account to regard them as belonging to it, and to go on working without change, calmly and evenly.

Only at the beginning of every matter is man free to resolve, free to decide where the *Omnipotent Power flowing through him* is to be guided, in what direction. He must then bear the consequences arising from the Power that was set in motion *in the direction willed by him.* In spite of this, many persist in asserting that even so man has no free will if he is subject to fate.

This foolishness is only meant to serve as a narcotic, or to be grudging submission to something inevitable, a discontented resignation, but mainly a self-excuse; for each of these consequences falling back on him had a beginning, and at *this beginning* the cause of the subsequent effect lay in a previous *free decision* by man.

This free decision has at some time or other preceded *every* reciprocal action, thus every fate! With the first decision man has each time produced or created something in which he himself has to live afterwards, sooner or later. *When* this will happen, however, varies greatly. It can still be in the same earth-life in which his first decision made the beginning for it, but it can equally well happen in the ethereal world, when the material body has been laid aside, or later still in yet another material earth life.

The variations are not important here, they do not free man from the consequences. He carries the connecting threads with him continually, until he is redeemed from them, that is to say "detached" through the final effect that ensues through the Law of Reciprocal Action.

Thus in the mighty machinery of the Universe there are many things which contribute to how man "fares," but there is nothing to which man has not himself first given cause.

How often does one hear otherwise very sensible people say: "It is incomprehensible to me that God should allow such a thing!"

But it is incomprehensible that man can speak thus. How small they imagine God to be with this remark. They prove thereby that they think of God as an *arbitrarily acting God.*

But God does not at all directly intervene in all these small and great cares of men, such as wars, misery and other earthly matters. From the very beginning He has woven into Creation His perfect Laws, which automatically carry out their incorruptible work so that all is accurately fulfilled, forever taking effect uniformly, thus preventing any preference as well as any prejudice, an injustice being impossible.

But one of the principle mistakes so many people make is that they only judge according to matter, regarding themselves as the center therein, and taking into consideration only *one* earth-life, whereas in reality they already have *several* earth-lives behind them. These, as well as the intervening times in the ethereal world, are equal to one *uniform* existence, through which the threads are tightly stretched without breaking.

Many are alarmed at this and afraid of what they still have to expect from the past through the reaction in accordance with these Laws.

But such are unnecessary worries for those who are in earnest about the good "volition" [free will decisions and actions]; *for in the self-acting Laws also lies at the same time the certain guarantee of mercy and forgiveness!*

With the firm beginning of the good volition, a *limit* is immediately set for the point where the chain of evil reactions must come to an end, [and also] another process of immense importance comes into force:

Through the continuing good volition in every thought and deed, a *constant reinforcement* also flows *retroactively* from the homogeneous Source of Power, so that the good becomes more and more firmly established in man himself, emerges from him, and first of all *forms accordingly the ethereal surrounding that envelopes him like a protective covering* in much the same way as the atmospheric layer round the earth affords a protection.

Now when evil reactions from the past return to this man to be redeemed, they *slide off the purity* of his surrounding or covering, and are thus deflected from him.

But should they nevertheless penetrate this covering, the evil radiations are either immediately disintegrated or at least appreciably weakened so that the harmful effect cannot manifest at all, or only to a very minor extent.

In addition, through the resulting *transformation,* the actual inner man [vibration] to whom the returning radiations are adjusted has also become much more *refined and lighter* through the continuous striving for the good volition, so that he no longer has any homogeneous affinity with the greater *density* of evil or base *currents.* Similar to the [radio] when it is not tuned in to the energy or frequency of the transmitter.

The natural consequences of this is that the denser currents, because they are of a different [waveform], cannot take hold of anything, and thus pass harmlessly through without evil effect.

Therefore set to work without delay! The Creator has placed everything in Creation into your hands. Make use of the time! Every moment holds disaster or gain for you.

Now, I have a theory concerning the concept of this person as it relates to the Law of Grace. See if it makes any sense to you.

Notice how he uses the familiar terms "currents" (as in electric) and "radiations" (waves or particles such as light) to describe the workings of Grace and the karmic Laws. Cayce also referred to the Spirit as being electrical:

Thus there are the *vibrations* of the electrical energies of the body, for Life itself is electrical. . ." (281-27)

Electricity or vibration is that same energy, same power, ye call God. Not that God is an electric light or an electric machine, but that vibration that is creative is of that same energy as life itself. (2828-4)

Know then that the force in nature that is called electrical is that same force as Creative, or God in action. (1299-1)

For this is the basis of materiality; for matter is that demonstration of the units of positive and negative energy, *when they become spiritual are they ONLY positive.* (412- 9)

Returning to Jesus and the resurrection then; was His "spiritual body" made up of positive electrical energy? Is this why it was not until the "sixth meeting" that He completed the "assembly" of His crucified body—"the conscious union with the sources of all power, of all force"— and was able to take food? Did He need "human time" in order to do this in accordance with the Laws of the material world? It is the conclusion I've come to in trying to interpret the readings on the subject.

So, both good and bad karma is first "activated" in a vibrational or electrical manner before it works its way with us. With regards to the bad karma, this obviously would return because of some harmful or immoral deed from the past. But it is not pure; it's kind of messy and therefore heavier or denser. Its current, or voltage, is lower than the highest possible voltage that was evident in Jesus Christ at His resurrection. If the person for whom the returning karma has changed for the good, this "lower voltage" cannot penetrate the higher, stronger type, so it sort of bounces off. Then, it seems to follow, returning good karma can thus increase or raise the voltage or vibrations of the individual in a reverse way since it has more "power."

There are many passages in the Bible that say "all power" has been granted to Jesus Christ. Why are we told this? Why is it claimed that the Christ Soul is the One we should look to for help—the One in which we can "meet every trial"—that is the Way for human souls to receive Grace and the love of God? The Cayce readings repeat this over and over.

I feel the Cayce source had extraordinary perception when conversing on the life and teachings of Jesus. There seemed to be a special rapport or connection. This, perhaps, because Cayce himself was a religious man and a devout Christian, as were many of his supporters.

For example, the following reading was offered spontaneously by Edgar Cayce in 1932 at the conclusion of a physical reading after the usual suggestion for him to wake up had been given three times:

> The Lord's Supper—here with the Master—see what they had for supper—boiled fish, rice with leaks, wine, and loaf. One of the pitchers in which it was served was

broken—the handle was broken, as was the lip of same.

The whole robe of the master was not white, but pearl gray—all combined into one—the gift of Nicodemus to the Lord.

The better looking of the twelve, of course, was Judas, while the younger was John—oval face, dark hair, smooth face—only one with the short hair. Peter, the rough and ready—always that of very short beard, rough, and not altogether clean; while Andrew's is just the opposite—very sparse, but inclined to be long more on the side and under the chin—long on the upper lip—his robe always near gray or black, while his clouts or breeches were striped; while those of Philip and Bartholemew were red and brown.

The master hair is most red, inclined to be curly in portions yet not feminine or weak—*strong,* with heavy piercing eyes that are blue or steel-gray.

His weight would be at least a hundred and seventy pounds. Long tapering fingers, nails well kept. Long nail, though, on the left little finger. (1315-1)

At this point, I would like to interrupt this captivating narration with a rare fragment of information from another source that expands on this description of Jesus and would be difficult for me to exclude.

LETTER TO TIBERIAS

Few people are aware that there is in existence today, in the Archives of Rome, a description of Christ. It is contained in a report written nearly two thousand years ago by a Roman, Publius Lentulus, to his Emperor, Tiberias. It reads:

There appeared in Palestine a man who is still living and whose power is extraordinary. He has the title given him of Great Prophet, his disciples call him "Son of God." He raises the dead and heals all sorts of diseases.

He is a tall, well proportioned man, and there is an air of severity in his countenance which at once attracts the love and reverence of those who see him. His hair is the color of new wine from the roots to the ears, and thence to the shoulders it is curled and falls down to the lowest part of them. Upon the forehead it parts in two after the manner of Nazarenes. His forehead is flat and fair, his face without blemish or defect, and adorned with a graceful expression. His nose and mouth are very well proportioned, his beard is thick and the color of his hair. His eyes are grey and extremely lively.

In his reproofs he is terrible, but in his exhortations and instructions, amiable and courteous. There is something wonderfully charming in his face with a mixture of gravity. He is never seen to laugh, but has been observed to weep. He is very straight in stature, his hands large and spreading, his arms are very beautiful.

He talks little, but with great quality, and is the handsomest man in the world.

And finally, to complete our portrait of Jesus, we have the following from another reading:

Q: Please give a physical description of Jesus.
A: A picture (of Jesus) that might be put on canvas. . .would be entirely different from all those that have depicted the face, the body, the eyes, the cut of the chin, and the lack entirely of the Jewish or Aryan profile. For these were clear, clean, ruddy. Hair almost like that of David; a golden brown, yellow red." (5354)

Now to return to the Cayce reading on the Lord's Supper:

Merry—even in the hour of trial. Joking—even in the moment of betrayal.

The sack is empty. Judas departs.

The last is given of the wine and loaf, with which he gives the emblems that should be so dear to every follower of Him. Lays aside his robe, which is all of one piece—girds the towel about His waist, which is dressed with linen that is blue and white. Rolls back the folds, kneels first before John, James, then Peter—who refuses.

Then the dissertation as to "He that would be the greatest would be servant of all."

The basin is taken as without handle, and is made of wood. The water is from the gherkins, that are in the wide-mouth shibboleths that stand in the house of John's father, Zebedee.

And now comes "It is finished."

They sing the ninety-first Psalm—"He that dwelleth in the secret place of the Most High shall abide under the shadow of the Almighty. I will say of the Lord, He is my refuge and my fortress; my God; in Him I trust."

He is the musician as well, for He uses the harp.

They leave for the garden.

The narrative proceeds from another reading:

Those periods in the garden—these become that in which the great trial is shown. . .and the fulfilling of all that had been in the purpose and the desire in the entrance into the world.

The trial [before the high priests and Pilate]—this was not with the pangs of pain, as so oft indicated, but rather glorying in the opportunity of taking upon self that which would RIGHT man's relationship to the Father, in that man, through his free will, had brought sin into activities of the children of God. Here HIS SON was bringing redemption through the shedding of blood that they might be free. (5749-10)

And so the perfected Christ Soul was a willing volunteer who, in order to assist our souls in our evolutionary development, took it upon Himself to enter our world as Jesus, and be crucified. Thus, by the life lived, and His sacrifice, He made His will one with God, and becomes the Way.

I know you have heard the expressions "enter the Light" or "surround yourself with the Light" and so forth. The Cayce readings suggest surrounding oneself with the "Christ Consciousness."

These various expressions seem to be saying the same thing. By following the example that Jesus showed us, the Way, we can sort of "plug into" the only positive Christ electrical circuitry, His electro*positive* power supply. We thereby charge our ethereal voltage with His power, which in turn surrounds and protects us. The New Covenant and Grace.

The Destiny of the Soul
(and that place known as Hell?)

One might ask, "Why should we humans care about the soul's destiny or its purpose; what's in it for me—is not the soul immortal?"

It seems possible that God is interested in the development of the soul. But why should this concern Him? Is this not an automatic process that He set in motion, and will eventually come to fruition when the perfected soul returns to Him? Some believe the answer may be no, but you may draw your own conclusions as I present the information. Much "New Age" thinking seems to be along this line.

If it's an automatic "given," then why the life of Jesus, His message, and His sacrifice—were they still necessary?

But if Creation is the Will of God in manifestation, and the soul has free will, then the evidence seems to indicate it is the duty of the soul to make its will one with God. And further, what are the *consequences* if it doesn't?

There may be a great misconception here. Many rely on the passage from First Corinthians, repeated often in the Cayce readings. For example, from reading 1347-1: "For hath it not been given that the Lord thy God hath not willed that any soul should perish, but He hath prepared with every temptation, a way of escape." If glossed over, without dissecting the passage or meaning of the words, it can be comforting. Is The Way of escape our choice?

Consider the spirit as a spark of God, sent out in the beginning from the spiritual realm. It is bestowed with a mind, and a free will; for these are the tools it will need to *experience* Creation, a manifestation of God's will. Some refer to God's Creation as the "superconscious" mind. One source has described God as the Artist, and the Painting as His Creation. And this Painting is a

123

never-ending Work—always in motion, ever changing. But the Laws that govern it are unchangeable—perfect in all respects.

The reason God sent out the spirit spark in the first place, according to the Cayce readings, is God's desire for companionship. It is His intent that the spirit spark become *conscious of itself,* make its will one with His, and as a fully developed individualized spirit, become a co-creator with God.

Once the spirit is launched into *self-conscious creation* with its tools on board, its pattern expands, and it becomes a developing soul, consisting of spirit, mind, and free will.

As part of this process the soul enters the material world which consists of *ethereal* matter and physical matter, the ethereal being the much greater part, and not limited to time and space. It takes on the ethereal cloak, and with its mind and free will as companions, proceeds on its course.

It may enter a physical body, or develop in other planes or spheres. It needs the ethereal cloak in order to function, and, if it chooses, inhabit a physical body.

It now has a slightly different form or pattern, and if it chooses a physical body, the pattern expands more—it takes on additional baggage.

The descriptive term *entity* seems to be used in the Cayce readings to delineate the circumstances of the soul that has decided to inhabit a physical body. Possibly because, at death, the soul absorbs its earthly experiences, both good and bad. Thus its *ethereal vibration is different than it had been at physical birth.* Its environment in the "beyond" is now subject to its vibration which is composed of the total combination of the many free will choices it acted out while on earth. What some refer to as *character* in a human being is part of the volition of the soul. Thus the soul is lighter or heavier and gravitates (yes, there is a sort of "ethereal law of gravity") to that level or sphere as ordained by its vibration. It is granted the opportunity to be closely associated with other souls of a similar volition. Just think, constantly associating with souls just like you! One should consider—would they define their new dwelling place in the "beyond" as heaven, or hell, or somewhere in between?

So as the soul develops in a positive manner, it becomes lighter and lighter and is eventually able to enter the spiritual realm of heaven.

We humans have been told that we are three-dimensional: body, mind, and soul. We know the body, with its demands; we know the intellectual (conscious) mind, its limitations and ability to choose (i.e., conscious free will); but the soul escapes us, although we're sure it's there. And our soul, with its own mind and free will (our subconscious), may see things differently. It seems we are meant to understand how all this meshes and works; the Laws of Creation. Otherwise, why is the urge to learn and investigate within all of us? One Cayce reading puts it as follows:

Many say that you have no consciousness of having a soul—yet the very fact that you hope, that you have a desire for better things, the very fact that you are able to be sorry or glad, indicates an activity of the mind that takes hold upon something that is not temporal in nature—something that passes not away with the last breath that is drawn but that takes hold upon the very sources of its beginning—the soul—that which was made in the image of your Maker—not your body, no—not your mind, but your soul was in the image of your Creator." (281-41)

The original choice to enter physical matter, and the eventual decision to make the *intuitive* (soul) mind subservient to the conscious *intellect* (the tree of knowledge?) may not have been intended or predestined. Some believe, or have surmised, that the spirit rebelled, and once this happened the readings state, "and as man's concept became to that point wherein man walked not after the ways of the Spirit but after the desires of the flesh sin entered —that is, away from the Face of the Maker, see? And death then became man's portion, SPIRITUALLY, see? For the physical death existed from the beginning." (900-227)

Of course, there are many teachings that claim the soul decided to manipulate physical consciousness. Perhaps it could do a better job at creating than God. This may be the references to the fallen angels, and the many admonishments in the Bible and other religious teachings to repent.

What caused the first influences in the earth that brought

selfishness? The desire to be as gods, in that rebellion became the order of the mental forces in the soul; and sin entered. (5753-1)

So the often-used term *to save souls* makes sense. As the soul develops toward "spirituality," it becomes lighter, less dense. As its will becomes one with God's will, it ascends and its ethereal cloak dissolves—no more excess baggage. The soul enters the spiritual realm and becomes a companion, an individualized, self-conscious entity, with all its perfected attributes. Also, since each soul's experiences are somewhat different in the vast system of Creation, it brings a special, exclusive talent, different from all others, so it may express it in Creation, and participate with it throughout eternity.

We are completely in charge of our own destinies. Only we can create our own Heaven or Hell by our actions. And these actions include our thoughts, for thoughts are deeds. Thoughts are matter too—ethereal matter. They send out electrical-like currents, or waves that help to mold ethereal substance. Thoughts are also absorbed by our spirit and in some manner recorded on the soul's tape machine for some unspecified future playback. We cannot blame others for our suffering, nor can others take credit for our good fortune.

So the perfected soul enters heaven, the kingdom of God. However, in Matthew 7:21 Jesus says, "Not everyone who says to me, 'Lord, Lord,' will enter the kingdom of heaven, but only he who does the will of my Father who is in heaven."

And who can describe heaven? The concepts are many. I am reminded of the story related by the British statesman, Lloyd George, quoted by Dr. MacGregor: ". . .recalling his boyhood years, he said 'that he had been more afraid of heaven than of hell, for he had pictured it as a place of perpetual Sundays with perpetual chapel services presided over by God who, with the assistance of hosts of angels, would be keeping close check on everyone's attendance.' This, he said, 'made him an atheist for ten years.'" The doctrine of reincarnation persuaded him to reshape his thinking.

At the present time we are still in the process of constructing our souls. Our everyday decisions and actions are the materials we use.

The "Grail Message" suggests that each stage of the structure is meant to be completed in conformity with God's time frame.

It further suggests that the combination of the choices we make in this regard, *eventually create an inertia that is more and more difficult to reverse.* The more good that we do, the easier it gets, and of course, the less we do the harder it gets. Like the fruit on a tree, we must ripen in an orderly fashion and fulfill our purpose, as ordained by God's Laws, or fall to the ground and decompose, returning to the soil.

Not by desire does the Father permit us to experience long suffering, one of the fruits of the spirit, whether on this side or the other. He allows this suffering to force us to think and to change our volition.

And all this occurs exactly in accordance with Creation's Laws. If the soul decomposes, it is totally dissolved because of wrong choices, and all that remains is the unconscious spirit energy of the soul, the same spirit spark sent out in the beginning by God. The spirit, as part of the First Cause, cannot die; it returns, submerging like a drop of water in the boundless, unconscious spiritual ocean. It is no longer conscious of itself. No more mind—no more free will. This, according to many sources, is the true meaning of Hell and Damnation, the worst of consequences. All that effort for nothing.

To support this scenario, a few quotes from the Bible and the readings are offered for your consideration.

> But if men are bound in chains, held fast by cords of affliction, He tells them what they have done—that they have sinned arrogantly. He makes them listen to correction and commands them to repent of their evil. If they obey and serve Him, they will spend the rest of their days in prosperity and their years in contentment. But if they do not listen, they will *perish* and will cross the river without knowledge. (Job 36:8-12)

> For God so loved the world that he gave His only begotten Son that whoever believes in Him shall not *perish* but have eternal life. (John 3:16)

My sheep listen to my voice; I know them, and they follow me. I give them eternal life and they shall never *perish*; no one can snatch them out of my Father's hand. (John 10:27-28)

But do not forget this one thing, dear friends: With the Lord a day is like a thousand years, and a thousand years like a day. The Lord is not slow in keeping His promise, as some understand slowness. He is patient with you, not wanting anyone to perish, but everyone to come to repentance. (2nd Peter 3:8-9)

During a reading concerning the prophecies of the great pyramid, Cayce was asked, "What is the meaning of the empty sarcophagus (coffin)? He answered that the meaning of death would be made clear (perhaps during this time if the pyramid does, in fact, contain predictions for this period as some researchers have concluded).

I think this statement may have had a much deeper meaning than simply the understanding and acceptance of the doctrine of reincarnation.

Can the soul "perish"? It certainly is not meant to. But let me offer a few excerpts from the Cayce readings to assist in the debate:

. . .Yet various phases by the activity of the entity as it has done or does that about Creative Forces which gives life, light and immortality, the expression of an entity that may be its own. Yet if it separates itself from the Creative Forces it must *eventually* become *null* and *void;* for it separates itself from life itself. (633-2)

. . .No urge exceeds the will of the individual entity, that gift from and of the Creative Forces that separates man, even the Son of man, from the rest of creation. Thus it is made to be ever as one with the Father, knowing itself and yet one with the Father, never losing its identity. *For to lose its identity is death indeed*—separation from the Creative Force. The soul may never be lost, for it returns to the One Force, *but knows not itself to be itself any more.* (3357-1)

Q: Must each soul continue to be reincarnated in the earth until it reaches perfection, or are some souls lost?

A: Can God lose itself, if God be God, or is it [the soul] submerged, or is it as has been given, carried into the universal soul or consciousness? The soul is not lost; the individuality of the soul that separates itself is lost. The reincarnation or the opportunities [other realms] are continuous until the soul has of itself become as entity in its whole or has submerged itself. (826-8)

Q: When a soul, by the reason of wrong development banishes itself from its Maker, does that mean it may never return to find its Maker?

A: Banished means separated, cast out, and in such conditions has lost its relationship to the First Cause and is only exemplified, manifested, shown, or has its being in the developing, retarding, or existences, of other souls. (900-10)

When there is such a diffusion of consciousness as to change, alter or create a direction for an activity of any influence (that has taken on consciousness of matter) to waver it from its purpose for being in consciousness—it loses its individual identity. (826-11)

For hath he not given, "They that turn their face far from me, I will blot them out." (1977-1)

Finally, returning to First Corinthians:

For He thy Father, thy God, hath not willed that any soul should perish. Thus the soul that separates itself from the Maker doeth so in spite of the Maker, and is as that free will that hath been given to each soul, that is the birthright of each soul. (1257-1)

So, if there is a possibility that the soul can perish, some may have a serious problem. Actually *two* problems. (I know, "Speak for yourself!" I'm just hoping that a statement in reading 5284-1 is from a *very high source:* "It is never too late to mend thy ways.")

The first problem is obviously the "death" of the soul. And although some may say "so what, so I lose my identity," it is doubtful they seriously believe this. In desperation, many a disbeliever turns to God in his waning moments! And a prayer of supplication *can* be the seed that takes root in the soul mind and starts to grow in a spiritual direction.

One of the most often used statements in the readings is "mind is the builder." This refers to "gnosticism," which was a "philosophical and religious system [1st to 6th century] teaching that knowledge rather than faith was the key to salvation." (*Funk & Wagnalls.*) Cayce was asked: "Is gnosticism the closest form of Christianity to that which is given through this source?" He answered: "This is a parallel, and was the commonly accepted one until there were the attempts to take short cuts. And there are none in Christianity." (5749-14)

So if knowledge, using our conscious minds as the builders, is the key for the salvation of our souls, then there isn't much chance we will find the answers unless we seek them. And this isn't as difficult as some would have you believe. God's Laws, the Universal Laws, are fairly simple and straightforward. Anyone can learn these Laws. God does not just dish them out to a select few because of their positions, rank, or education. He does not discriminate against any soul. Learning the Universal Laws is important, as Cayce reading 900-17 states: "Jesus. . .only used the Universal Law. . ." (900-17)

The second problem is a result of the first. God's Laws provide opportunities that we are compelled to experience; like it or not! He permits us to suffer with the intent that this will further our development in the right direction—toward the Spiritual Realm. But as previously surmised, it's possible that the soul's development may not go on indefinitely. It has to someday return "home." This may be why the readings encourage us to observe Mother Nature, the ever-changing material part of Creation in strict accordance with Creation's Laws. After all, if something is "perishable," it is subject to decay.

In another reading, Cayce was asked, "What is meant by banishment of a soul from its Maker?" Answer: "Of the will as given in the beginning to choose for self as in the earthly plane, all insufficient matter is cast unto Saturn, to work out its own salvation as would be termed in the *word*. The entity or individual banishes itself, or its soul, which is the entity." (3744-2)

On several occasions the readings state the souls that have misbehaved are banished to the dimension known as Saturn for "remolding"—not a very agreeable term!

In August 1938, a father requested a physical reading (1671-1) for his 20-year-old son who was afflicted with strabismus (crossed eyes). While the stenographer was recording his words, Cayce had a dream-like experience which he narrated after he returned to his waking consciousness:

> I thought I was on Saturn. The ring around it was like a shield, and was the place where entities learned that they couldn't go all the way around the ring like they could on earth. . .to Saturn go those who would renew or begin again; or who have [much of the memory of the soul mind] blotted from their experience. . .(945-1)

Should we conclude that to "perish" or to be "banished to Saturn," are one in the same? The word *banish* seems to exclude the possibility of a reversal—*finis!* Is this part of the procedure—the itinerary for "remolding?" Somehow, I get the feeling that a soul landing on the surface, the dimension, or the realm referred to as Saturn may not be a pleasant experience!

The great mechanism of God's Laws in the world of matter, on both this side and the other, will offer every soul many opportunities on a multitude of spheres or planes so that it may polish its soul. As for me, I'm not anxious to open my mail and find marching orders from the Commander in Chief mandating my presence for an extended tour of duty on Planet Saturn, and without leave!

The time may be ripe for humanity to change its ways. From reading 5148-2: "What is needed in the earth today? That the sons of men be *warned* that the day of the Lord is near at hand, and that those who have been and are unfaithful must meet themselves in those things which come to pass in their experience."

Another dilemma! I thought "the day of the Lord" would at least signal a less stressful existence! Why are we being warned? To what does this warning apply? Is it the Last Judgment? Well, let's move on to the next chapter to see if we can find an answer to this perplexing question.

But first, I want you to know that I struggled long and hard in my mind, and debated with myself, as to whether I should even include the "earth changes" information in this compilation. In addition, I gave it to a dozen or so friends to read and asked their opinion. Some said a definite yes—some were neutral, and a few thought it might be too much. I don't want you or your friends to think I'm a doom-and-gloomer or an alarmist. But here again, what right do I have to leave it out? I'm not saying these predicted changes are etched in stone—I'm not a pyramid expert or, for that matter, an expert in anything.

A lot of doom and gloom has been predicted, and I don't feel it is my prerogative to omit certain information on the subject because it is unpleasant—or in the opinion of some, preposterous and unscientific. Others can draw their own conclusions regarding credibility and acceptability. I'm not trying to convince anyone concerning the accuracy or truth of this information. The only "truth" I'm attempting to present is the fact that these statements, theories, predictions, and various prophecies do exist, they're "in the world" for whatever reason, and to learn of them is an experience in awareness.

As Patrick Henry put it so well:

It is natural for man to indulge in the illusions of hope. We are apt to shut our eyes against a painful truth...Are we disposed to be the number of those, having eyes, see not, and having ears, hear not the things which so nearly concern our temporal salvation? For my part, whatever anguish of spirit it may cost, I am willing to know the whole truth, to know the worst, and to provide for it.

For me this is nothing more than an "exposure exercise" that may be of some use to someone. My foremost reason for putting all of this in writing was to give you and Timmy a sort of dad's-awareness inheritance. Certainly, neither of you are obligated to embrace any of it. Someday, I'm sure we will all know whether there is any truth to all of this, or not.

While reading these various predictions and prophecies, please keep in mind that, if there is any truth to them, there is still hope.

And so, Amy, as you read the next chapter, try to keep in mind the following excerpts from "A Prophetic Poem," written by Thomas Sugrue, author of *There is a River*.

. . .When the 20th century shall have passed away and the sign of the God-man is in the sky; peace shall reign upon the earth and no man shall hate his brother.

Neither shall there be war, nor pestilence, nor poverty, nor any other of the shameful things which man has done unto himself since first he knew shame. . .

Nations that are great shall have perished and all men, seeking to be brothers shall have put their hands to a common pledge and raised up a single force to rule them—the force of Wisdom.

. . .For Wisdom brings peace, and teaches love, and sets the face of man toward His Spirit.

And in that time these things shall be and the earth and the sky and the sea shall open to man their secrets.

Sound from heaven shall bend itself to the ears of man that he may hear the music of the spheres, and understand the rhythms of his soul.

And through all the land, Love like a famished child, shall sit down to a feast and rise up filled with joy.

No debts shall be made yet all promises shall be fulfilled.

Death shall come to meet no man. All men shall go to meet death

And God shall be pleased, and tent the rose with a deeper red, and raise the skylark in the sky.

The New Age "Birth Pangs"

The catastrophic weather, earthquakes, floods—the turmoil and strife—and much more that Cayce and others have predicted are beyond the imagination. And Cayce predicted them to begin in 1958 and increase in intensity into the next century. They seem to be a reflection of the Bible prophecies that people point to for the "birth pangs of the New Age":

> The time is coming when you will hear the noise of battle near at hand and the news of battles far away; see that you are not alarmed. Such things are bound to happen; but the end is still to come. For nation will make war upon nation, kingdom upon kingdom; there will be famines and earthquakes in many places. With all these things the birth pangs of the New Age begin. (Matthew 24:6-7-8)

> For there will be great distress, unequaled from the beginning of the world until now—and never to be equaled again. . . (Matthew 24:21)

> Immediately after the distress of those days, the sun will be darkened, and the moon will not give its light; the stars will fall from the sky, and the heavenly bodies will be shaken. . . (Matthew 24:29) (More on this later.)

> When you hear of wars and revolutions, do not be frightened. These things must happen first, but the end will not come right away...Nation will rise against nation, and kingdom against kingdom. There will be great earthquakes, famines and pestilences in various places, and fearful events and great signs from heaven. (Luke 21:9-11)

> There will be signs in the sun, moon, and stars. On the

134

earth, nations will be in anguish and perplexity at the roaring and tossing of the sea. Men will faint from terror, apprehensive of what is coming on the world, for the heavenly bodies will be shaken. (Luke 21:25-26)

You must face the fact: the final age of this world is to be a time of troubles. Men will love nothing but money and self; they will be arrogant, boastful and abusive; with no respect for parents, no gratitude, no piety, no natural affection; they will be implacable in their hatreds, scandal-mongers, intemperate and fierce, strangers to all goodness, traitors, adventurers, swollen with self-importance. They will be men who put pleasure in the place of God, men who preserve the outward form of religion, but are a standing denial of its reality. (Paul's second letter to Timothy, 3:1-5)

Paul had a high regard for prophecy. In his first letter to the Corinthians (14:1-4) he instructs them:

Put love first, but there are other gifts of the Spirit at which you should aim also, and above all, prophecy. When a man is using the language of ecstasy he is talking with God, not with men, for no man understands him; he is no doubt inspired, but he speaks mysteries. On the other hand, when a man prophesies, he is talking to men, and his words have power to build, they stimulate and encourage.

So prophecy is a gift of the Spirit. However, in the first letter of John (4:1) is the warning: "But do not trust any and every spirit, my friends; test the spirits, to see whether they are from God, for among those who have gone out into the world there are many prophets falsely inspired."

Today there are thousands of individuals "channeling" advice and information from who knows where! Their predictions cover everything imaginable under the sun. But very few have been checked out or documented. Reaching out into the ethereal world (or even the subconscious mind) for information is dependent upon many variables. When dealing with world prophecy, time frames can be very elusive for several reasons. And, of course, setting dates for a fixed future event that doesn't occur on schedule tends to discredit all prophecy.

In Matthew 24:36 Jesus says, "But about that day and hour no one knows, not even the angels in heaven, not even the Son; only the Father."

Edgar Cayce was asked in 1935, "When is this likely to occur?" He answered, "As to times and places and seasons, as it has indeed been indicated in the greater relationships that have been established by the prophets and sages of old—and especially as given by Him, as to the day and the hour, who knoweth? No one save the Creative Forces." (417-6)

I mentioned that there are differing opinions as to "if" or "when" or "where" these catastrophic events would take place. In 1932 someone asked Cayce, "What form will they take?" He answered:

> . . .for as understood—or should be by the entity—there are those conditions that in the activity of individuals, in line of thought and endeavor, oft keep many a city and many a land intact through their application of the spiritual Laws in their association with individuals. Tendencies in the hearts and souls of men are such that these [upheavals] may be brought about. For as often indicated through these channels oft, it is not the world, the earth, the environs about it nor the planetary influences that rule man. Rather does man—by his compliance with divine Law—bring order out of chaos; or by his disregard of the associations and the Laws of divine influence, bring chaos and destructive forces into his experience. (416-7)

And in 1941 another person asked: "What can we do to counteract such happenings?" Answer: "Make known the trouble where it lies, that they who have forgotten God must right about face." (3976-26)

Has humanity done an about-face? Some think so, others don't! I guess it has to do with intuition, or belief, or denial, or whatever.

These readings seem to be saying that it is next to impossible to set dates for any given event in our physical world, especially "earth changes." Yet Cayce and others have done it with notable success. Without doubt, there have been plenty of misses also!

If it's true that everything that takes place in physical matter is first formed in the denser astral matter of ethereal substance, and that our thoughts and actions shape the astral matter, then we are to some extent responsible for the behavior of Mother Nature. The more negative "vibes" we ship to the other side, the more cataclysmic the reaction on earth. The astral matter becomes darker and heavier, and at some point it has to release the burden by delivering the freight.

In the recent book *Beyond Prophecies and Predictions*, by Moria Timms, is the following teaching by the Japanese prophet Meishu Sama, from earlier in this century:

> . . .human actions and speech of a violent, destuctive or negative nature create clouds in the spiritual realms which gather near their source until (like rain) they are finally dissipated by natural law in the form of turbulent weather or disasters. . .the Earth is going to have to face "a mighty upheaval, the greatest catacysm in all history."

Prophets have always found themselves in a predicament when it comes to forecasting events. They are given messages in order to warn humanity to change their ways or else. The dark, dense astral matter is on the loading dock and will soon be shipped unless it can be made lighter and less dense by the ethereal infiltration of humanity's positive actions. Once it is shipped, its too late. The exact arrival time of the material may be difficult to determine, but the contents of consequences cannot be returned for a refund. So when a prophet or psychic predicts that a certain event will happen on a specific date, because of the no-time problem in the ethereal, it's hard to tell if the date given is the shipping date or the delivery date.

Also, while our package is en route, it can still be charged with positive vibes, and the effects of its contents lightened. Maybe a 5.3 quake instead of a 7.5 shaker.

In the meantime, our prophet is stuck in a no-win situation. If the event occurs, obviously he (or she) is not very popular. Many times they are even blamed. If the package is delayed in route for some reason, then the prophet's reputation is at risk. Of course, if people do heed the warnings and change, then the prophet is dead wrong! Just another doom-sayer.

In Matthew 24:32-33, Jesus says, "Learn a lesson from the fig tree. When its tender shoots appear and are breaking into leaf, you know that summer is near. In the same way, when you see all these things, you may know that the end is near, at the very door." In Luke 21:36 He says, "Be always in the watch, and pray that you may be able to escape all that is about to happen. . ."

And if true, it is some kind of happening! In 1934 a Cayce reading states "...That some are due and will occur is written, as it were, but—as we find—as to specific date or time in the present this may not be given." (270-32)

So it appears, in trying to figure all of this out, we are meant to watch world events as they unfold during the next decade—to look for clues—to compare—and to make as many connections as possible.

For instance: "When you hear of wars and revolutions. . ." (Luke 21:9)—this prophecy could be referring to the former Yugoslavia, South Africa, Somalia, Rwanda, and other African countries, Haiti, Armenia, the many republics of the former Soviet Union, Israel, and Palestine, Lebanon, Northern Ireland, Peru and other South American countries, et cetera, et cetera! New ones are cropping up all the time.

And it seems that some have become concerned. A recent headline in our local paper reads "Peace On Earth: An Elusive Goal." The article goes on to state, "Depending on how you keep score, from 30 to 100 wars are being fought."

"Famines and pestilences in various places...(Luke 21:11). Tens of thousands of people around the world die every day from illnesses caused by the lack of food. And thousands more suffer from malnutrition. And some futurists claim that new diseases popping up, new bacteria, are an example of the predicted pestilences. Well, you get the idea; so if you're concerned, "watch and pray"—the answers should come to you.

In the late 1950s, a geologist wrote a booklet about Cayce's predictions called "Earth Changes." Shortly before his death in 1982, Edgar Cayce's son, Hugh Lynn, did a final update concerning the earth changes readings, which included the following.

Edgar Cayce had a dream on the night of March 3, 1936, while returning to Virginia Beach from Detroit by train. He had been arrested and jailed in Detroit for breaking the law—that is—giving readings! He was despondent and discouraged and was doubting the accuracy of his readings—all of those awful predictions about California falling into the sea, and the many others that you will soon be reading as we proceed.

In the appendix section of the *Earth Changes Update* booklet, Hugh Lynn asks the question, "Will the earth changes really come to pass?" He then states the following:

This question was probably a *burning one* of the psychic [Edgar Cayce] through whom the predictions came. It is understandable, therefore, that he might dream about "his" prophecies—about their meaning and about their veracity.

He had been born again in 2100 A.D. in Nebraska. The sea apparently covered all of the Western part of the country, as the city where he lived was on the coast. The family name was a strange one. At an early age as a child he declared himself to be Edgar Cayce who lived two hundred years before.

Scientists, men with long beards, little hair, and thick glasses were called to observe the child. They decided to visit the places he said he had been born, lived, and worked—in Kentucky, Alabama, New York, Michigan, and Virginia Beach. Taking the child with them the group of scientists visited these places in a long, cigar-shaped, metal flying ship which moved at high speed.

Water covered part of Alabama. Norfolk, Virginia had become an immense seaport. New York had been destroyed either by war or an earthquake and was being rebuilt. Industries were scattered over the countryside. Most of the houses were of glass.

Many records of Edgar Cayce's work were discovered and collected. The group returned to Nebraska, taking the records with them for study.

On the 30th of June, 1936, a reading was given in which an interpretation of the dream-experience was requested. The answer was as follows:

These experiences, as has oft been indicated, come to the body in those manners in which there may be help, strength, for periods when doubt or fear may have arisen. As in this experience, there were about the entity those influences which appeared to make for such a record of confusion as to appear to the material, or mental-minded as a doubting or fearing of those sources that [caused] the periods through which the entity was passing in that particular period.

And the vision was that there might be strength, that there might be an understanding, that though the moment may appear dark, though there may be periods of misinterpreting of purposes even these will be turned into that which will be the very proof itself in the experiences of the entity and those whom the entity might, whom the entity would, in its experience through the earth plane, help; and those to whom the entity might give hope and understanding.

This then is the interpretation. As has been given, "Fear not." Keep the faith; for those that be with thee are greater than those that would hinder. Though the very heavens fall, though the earth shall be changed, though the heavens shall pass, the promises in Him are sure and will stand—as in that day—as the proof of thy activity in the lives and hearts of thy fellow men.

For indeed in truth ye know, "As ye do it unto thy fellow man, ye do it unto thy God, to thyself." For, with self effaced, God may indeed glorify thee and make thee stand as one who is called for a purpose in the dealings, in the relationships with thy fellow man.

Be not unmindful that He is nigh unto thee in every trial, in every temptation, and hath not willed that thou shouldst perish.

Make thy will, then, one with His. Be not afraid.

That is the interpretation. That the periods from the material angle as visioned [dreamed] are to come to pass matters not to the soul but do thy duty today! Tomorrow will take care of itself.

These changes in the earth will come to pass, for the time and times and half times are at an end (Daniel 7:25, 12:7 and Revelation 12:14) and they begin these periods for the readjustments. For how hath He given? "The righteous shall inherit the earth." Hast thou, my brethern, a heritage in the earth? (294-185)

There is a circulating file on earth changes in the Cayce library in Virginia Beach. It contains references to about 80 readings that discuss earth changes in some manner, and of course there are others that aren't listed. The following quotes from the readings are the ones that are referred to most often:

Q: How soon will the changes in the earth's activities be apparent?

A: When there is the first breaking up of some conditions in the South Sea (that's South Pacific, to be sure), and those as apparent in the sinking or rising of that that's almost opposite same, or in the Mediterranean, and the Etna area, then we may know it has begun.

Q: How long before this will begin?

A: The indications are that some of these have already begun, yet others would say they are only temporary. We would say they have begun. . .

Q: Will there be any physical changes in the earth's surface in North America? If so, what sections will be affected and how?

A: All over the country we will find many physical changes of a minor or greater degree. The greater changes, as we will find, in America, will be the North Atlantic Seaboard Watch New York! Connecticut, and the like. (311-8, April 1932)

Q: What will be the type and extent of the upheaval in 1936?

A: The wars, [start of World War II] the upheavals in the interior of the earth, and the shifting of same [earth] by the differentiation in the axis as respecting the positions from the Polaris center. (5748-6, July 1932)

As to the changes physical again: The earth will be broken up in the western portion of America. The greater portion of Japan must go into the sea. The upper portion of

Europe will be changed as in the twinkling of an eye. Land will appear off the east coast of America. There will be upheavals in the Arctic and in the Antarctica that will make for the eruption of volcanos in the Torrid areas, and there will be the shifting then of the poles—so that where there have been those of a frigid or semi-tropical will become the more tropical, and moss and fern will grow. And these will begin in those periods in '58 to '98, when these will be proclaimed as the periods when His light will be seen again in the clouds.

The earth will be broken up in many places. The early portion will see a change in the physical aspect of the west coast of America. There will be open waters appear in the northern portions of Greenland. There will be new lands seen off the Caribbean Sea, and dry land will appear. . .South America will be shaken from the uppermost portion to the end, and in the Antarctica off Tierra Del Fuego, land, and a straight with rushing waters. (3976-15, January 1934)

Q: What are the primary causes of earthquakes. . .?
A: The causes of these, of course, are the movements about the earth; that is, internally—and the cosmic activity or influences of other planetary forces and stars and their relationships produce or bring about the activities of the elements of the earth; that is, the Earth, the Air, the Fire, the Water—and those combinations make for the replacements in the various activities." (270-35, January 1936)

Q: What great change or the beginning of what change, if any, is to take place in the earth in the year 2000 to 2001 A.D.?
A: When there is a shifting of the poles. Or a new cycle begins. (826-8, August 1936)

As to conditions in the geography of the world, of the country, changes here are gradually coming about. . .many portions of the east coast will be disturbed, as well as well as many portions of the west coast, as well as the central portion of the United States.

In the next few years [ethereal time or delivery delay?]

lands will appear in the Atlantic as well as in the Pacific. And what is the coast line of many a land will be the bed of the ocean. Even many of the battlefields of the present [1941] will be ocean, will be the seas, the bays, the lands over which the *new order* will carry on their trade one with another.

Portions of the now east coast of New York, or New York city itself, will in the main disappear. This will be in *another* generation, though; here, while the southern portions of Carolina, Georgia—these will disappear. This will be much sooner.

The waters of the [Great] lakes will empty into the Gulf [of Mexico], rather than the waterway over which such discussions have been recently made [St. Lawrence Seaway]. It would be well if the waterway were prepared, but not for that purpose for which it is in the present being considered.

Then the area where the entity is now located [Virginia Beach] will be among the safety lands, as will be portions of what is now Ohio, Indiana and Illinois and much of the southern portion of Canada and the eastern portion of Canada; while the western land, much of that is to be disturbed—in this land—as, of course, much in other lands.

Q: I have for many months felt that I should move away from New York city?

A: This is well, as indicated. There is too much unrest; there will continue to be the character of vibration that to the body will be disturbing, and eventually those destructive forces there—though these will be in the next generation.

Q: Will Los Angeles be safe?

A: Los Angeles, San Francisco, most all of these will be among those that will be destroyed before New York even. (1152-11, August 1941)

Q: Is this the period of the great tribulation spoken of in Revelation, or just the beginning, and if so just how can we help ourselves and others to walk more closely with God?

A: The great tribulation and periods of tribulation, as given, are the experiences of every soul, every entity. . .Man may become, with the people of the universe, ruler of any of the various spheres through which the soul passes in its experiences. Hence, as the cycles pass, as the cycles are passing, when there is come a time, a period of readjusting in the spheres, (as well as in the little earth, the little soul)—seek, then, as known, to present self spotless before that throne; even as *all* are commanded to be circumspect, in thought, in act, to that which is held by self as that necessary for the closer walk with Him. In that manner only may each atom (as man is an atom, or corpuscle, in the body of the Father) become a helpmeet with Him in bringing that to pass that all may be one with Him." (281-16, March 1933)

The Great Tribulation—from the book of Revelation! But there are many other terms used in the prophecies. The Hopi Indians use "Great Purification." Others use "Chastisement," "Retribution," and of course all refer to "Armageddon" and the "Final Judgment."

Tribulation is the term used by one gifted person when referring to the period from 1991 into the next century, and he further defines it as "a time period of *spiritual choosing*" as well as "great earth changes." His name is Gordon-Michael Scallion. The phenomenon that manifests through him is very similar to Cayce's.

He has given readings and seen visions of the Tribulation since the late 1970s. He began publishing a monthly newsletter, *The Earth Changes Report* in October 1991. He's also printed a map of the United States based on the information he's received showing a very different land mass for around the year 2000.

This map and his predictions are comparable to the pronouncements in the Cayce readings. And those that follow and document his vast number of predictions have concluded that he has approximately an 85-percent accuracy rate—about the same percentage Hugh Lynn Cayce claimed for his father.

So what could cause the occurrence of so many predicted catastrophic events? Like so many others, Scallion confirms that *we* do to some extent! That is, again, the combination of all of our thoughts, words, and deeds rise up to the ethereal world, take spiritual form, and then return to the physical environment as activity—"as above so below."

An Edgar Cayce reading states, "All one sees manifest in a material world is but a reflection or shadow of the real or spiritual life." (262-23) And as we are now aware, there are many planes or spheres or levels of existence—each occupied by souls in various degrees of development.

> There is no difference between the unseen world and that which is visible; save that in the unseen, so much greater expanse or space may be covered. (5754-3)

Also, according to many past and present individuals who claim to have the ability to travel and see the other side, the ethereal realm nearest the earth is dark grey in color from the effect of humanity's collective consciousness over thousands of years.

In the November 1993 *Earth Changes Report*, the following question was asked of Gordon-Michael Scallion: "Since we understand that conscious, focused attention on something has the ability to change it, to what extent can we as individuals and groups effect a mitigation of the Earth changes you see?" He answered:

> In the '70s the amount of positive consciousness required to bring about a change was relatively little. But, as we entered the end of the '80s, we entered into psychodynamic forces, psychic spiritual energy accelerations, which meant that whatever was in the collective consciousness was being amplified because of Earth and cosmic forces. So if the consciousness was loving and benevolent and following a spiritual ideal, then the planet would flourish and many things would be altered. The time frame of '87 through '89 was the crossover point which meant that each year afterwards it was going to require a lot more people—in the millions—to bring about positive change. There is not any event that I have predicted that can not be negated if enough people are living in harmony. It would now require 30 percent of the population of the United States [75 million people] to negate the events I have forecast.

This time period of '87 through '89 appears to straddle perfectly the date Jesus gave Dr. Ritchie. His travelog took place in 1943. Jesus said we had 45 years—1988!

When I recently talked with Dr. Ritchie, he said he felt the explosions he saw were nuclear and volcanic. He couldn't explain his vision of the military armies marching on the United States from the south (some speculate this vision meant waves of illegal immigration). He said his biggest worry is the fundamentalism movements evidenced in today's world.

And now let us return to the "Grail Message" to see if it has a shipping information "manifest." The following are a few excerpts from the essay "The Millennium":

> Admonitions through the prophets, then through the Son of God Himself, were not enough to change man and induce him to take the right course. He did not want to, and increasingly nourished his conceited idea of being a world-ruler, in which already lay hidden the germ for his inevitable downfall. This germ grew with his conceit, and prepared the catastrophes that must now be unleashed according to the Eternal Law in Creation, which man failed to recognize because of his conceited idea of being master prevented him from doing so.
>
> The sole cause of the coming horrors lies in the distortion of the Divine Laws through the false volition of human Spirits in Creation. . .
>
> That is also why the end could be foreseen already thousands of years ago; because owing to the wrongly-willed attitude of men it could not possibly come about any differently since the final result of anything that happens always remains strictly bound to the Divine Laws.

There is much more information from other sources on the theory that humanity in some way is the cause of the predicted earth changes. But another hypothesis has also been making the rounds for quite a while. It is from the Bible: "As soon as the distress of those days has passed, the sun will be darkened, the moon will not give her light; the stars will fall from the sky, and the celestial powers will be shaken. Then will appear in heaven the sign that heralds the Son of Man." (Matthew 24:29-30); and from the Cayce readings: ". . .And these [upheavals] will begin in those periods in '58 to '98, when these will be proclaimed as the periods when His Light will be seen again in the clouds." (3976-15)

Well, Amy, the explanation or rationale for these particular prophecies or scenarios is really difficult to fathom, as you well know. I appreciate all of your hard work and research in helping me assemble the information which follows about our yet-to-be-proven mysterious, unwelcome visitor from far out in space.

Planet X: Past, Present and Future Predictions

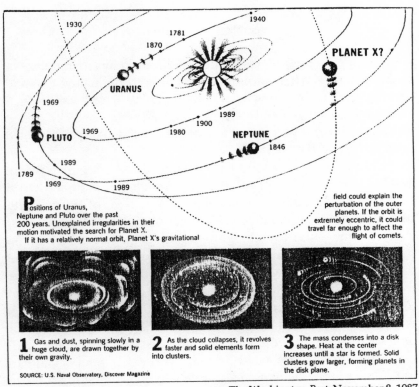

Positions of Uranus, Neptune and Pluto over the past 200 years. Unexplained irregularities in their motion motivated the search for Planet X. If it has a relatively normal orbit, Planet X's gravitational field could explain the perturbation of the outer planets. If the orbit is extremely eccentric, it could travel far enough to affect the flight of comets.

1 Gas and dust, spinning slowly in a huge cloud, are drawn together by their own gravity.

2 As the cloud collapses, it revolves faster and solid elements form into clusters.

3 The mass condenses into a disk shape. Heat at the center increases until a star is formed. Solid clusters grow larger, forming planets in the disk plane.

SOURCE: U.S. Naval Observatory, Discover Magazine

The Washington *Post*, November 8, 1987

The idea of a tenth planet has been popular since 1978, when the discovery of a moon of Pluto led astronomers to believe another large object was necessary to explain irregularities in the orbits of Neptune and Uranus. Some skepticism has been evident in the explanation of this hypothesis, as with any other, but the celestial mysteries that prompted the search, along with the possible ramifications that could occur should this planet enter our solar system, push some hopeful astronomers on, to find the mystery planet they call Planet X. The planet itself has been linked to the explanation of the demise of dinosaurs and has been included in futuristic predictions pertaining to the period of the coming millennium. Whatever the reader may conclude as fact or fantasy, possible or impossible, the possibilities for the existence of a tenth planet is an interesting and important prospect to investigate.

The Search For Planet X

Mercury, Venus, Mars, Jupiter, and Saturn have been known since antiquity. Their motion was visible to the naked eye and seen by ancient Greeks who called them planets or "wanderers." Uranus was discovered by Sir William Herschel in 1781, when he detected that it was fuzzy, not stellar (or star-like), and moved with respect to the stars.

Planetary motion was at first presumed to be regular. But in 1846, Englishman John Adams and French astronomer Urbain Le Verrier independently compared observations of Uranus with its ephemeris—a computed table describing a body's position at a given time—and found significant discrepancies. To explain the variation in the planet's position, they predicted that there had to be another planet whose gravitational force was affecting the motion of Uranus. The differences between the calculated and observed positions were approximately 100 seconds of arc, which is large by astronomical standards. Both Adams and LeVerrier had some trouble getting their fellow astronomers interested. LeVerrier finally convinced German astronomer Johann Galle to look. The prediction was so accurate that on the first night Galle detected the planet now known as Neptune.

A similar perception later led to the discovery of Pluto. Early in this century, Percival Lowill and W.C. Pickering analyzed the observed and predicted positions of Uranus and Neptune and found differences for Uranus of about 5 seconds of arc. The men concluded that there had to be yet another planet, or planets, in the solar system. In 1930, after Lowell's death, a new and more intensive search was initiated, and Pluto was found near the position he had predicted.

The discovery, however, had some missing links; it was not a completely conclusive and logical reason for the irregular motion of the outer planets. Lowell's prediction was based on a planet much farther from the sun and much more massive than Pluto. The gravitational influence of one planet on another is determined by mass and distance. The easy and accurate way to determine the mass of a planet is from the motion of a satellite. But the only known satellite of Pluto, Charon, was not discovered until 1978. Based on the knowledge we have today, Pluto is only about one five-hundredth the mass of Earth—much too small to be capable of detectably perturbing Uranus.

Pluto also varies from its predicted position; but the data are too modest and scant to be conclusive. Pluto is a 15th-magnitude object, 10,000 times too faint to be seen without a telescope. Observations have been available only since 1914—70 years out of an orbital period of 248. These observations have an uncertainty of approximately one second of arc. That range of uncertainty, combined with the short observation period, makes it impossible to calculate an accurate ephemeris.

The observations of Neptune, however, cover the period from 1846 to the present time, or 141 years out of the planet's 165-year period. These observations have been fit by ephemerides without difficulty. However, there is one enigmatic aspect to these observations. Approximately 10 years after an ephemeris has been calculated, Neptune no longer appears at the predicted locations. This has happened repeatedly since 1900 and continues today. No one can explain why this occurs. Some feel that perhaps a Planet X is deflecting Neptune from its course. But it is also possible that the observations will match predictions when they have covered a full orbital period.

Uranus continues to display irregularities in right ascension (it's location in the plane of the equator). No single ephemeris will fit the approximately 300 years of observations—or even those since 1830, when significant improvements in astronomy make data much more accurate. Since Uranus has an orbital period of about 80 years, almost two complete orbits are covered by the data. If observations from only one orbital period are used, an ephemeris fitting those observations can be calculated. But the same computations will not fit both orbits. Again, this could be the result of some external force such as Planet X. Others who disagree with the Planet X conclusion feel that observations before 1900 could have been subject to systematic error.

Robert S. Harrington, an astronomer at the U.S. Naval Observatory, is one scientist who believes in the possibility of a tenth planet. Because Pluto was discovered to have only a fraction of the mass of Earth, Harrington and other astronomers believe there must be another planet. The problem is finding it.

In 1929, Clyde Thombaugh began a search at the Lowell Observatory which resulted in the discovery of Pluto in 1930. He continued that search until 1946, covering a large part of the sky for objects as faint as the 16th magnitude. There are parts of the sky he did not cover, and it is possible that the planet could be fainter than the 16th magnitude.

Mr. Harrington in the past had searched for Planet X in areas that he estimated it would be located. New observations of the outer planets and their orbits have led Harrington to believe that he had been looking for the planet in the wrong places. According to an article in the April 27, 1990, edition of the Washington (D.C.) *Times*, Harrington stated that, "I've covered 6 percent of the sky and I'm now convinced it's the wrong 6 percent. . ." In that same article, Harrington had new calculations which focused his search in the constellation Centarus, which he said would be best observed during April and May of 1990. An associate of Mr. Harrington's was working at the Black Birch Astrometric Observatory in New Zealand in search of Planet X during those periods and did not find the mystery planet.

In April 1992, *Sky and Telescope* featured an article on Planet X, interviewing Clyde W. Tombaugh, the Emeritus Professor of Astronomy at New Mexico State University and the actual discoverer of Pluto. Tombaugh states in the article:

> . . . [I had] spent some 7,000 hours blinking plates over a period of 14 years, and I was conscious of seeing every

one of the 90 million star images. . .if anyone thinks I might have missed seeing a planet, he or she is welcome to reblink my plates. . .I covered two thirds of the entire sky. . .I have more confidence in the thoroughness of my own planet search than I have in the current Planet X predictions, which are largely based on marginal residuals in the observed orbits of the outer planets. . .[But even the skeptical opinion of Mr. Tombaugh could not totally eliminate the possibility of Planet X.] There is a very slim possibility that a 10th planet exists. The hunt should now be made in southern Aquarius or even Cetus. Fortunately, these regions are not rich in stars, and I think that such a search should be made. . .

The search continues to this very day for a tenth planet.In November 1991, there was a small article in *Popular Science* magazine that confirms the belief that Planet X is not a worn-out issue, but one that still sparks ones imagination and interest. The article states, "Some astronomers believe that there may also be a planet beyond Pluto in our own solar system, because historical records show wobbles in the orbits of both Uranus and Neptune— effects that can't be attributed to Pluto alone."

Our Future And Planet X

Planet X has also been an important component of predictions and prophecies concerning certain future events, which some feel will occur within the next ten to fifteen years. When mixing the certainty and unyielding proven facts of science with the speculated but quite possible predictions of the future, the reader should try to keep an open mind. Many discoveries and facts could not have happened without someone who had the courage to speculate and even make personal prophesies outside the ideas and norms of what society would consider valid or important. The information dealing with the future is difficult to prove for obvious reasons, but it is interesting to investigate yet another intriguing part of the Planet X mystery.

Thousands of books and articles have been written about this period and the coming millennium, the passing from the Age of Pisces into the Age of Aquarius. Much of this information deals with attempts to interpret coming events in correlation with the predictions from Bible prophecies and from latter-day seers such as the popular sixteenth-century French physician, Michel de Nostredame, more commonly known by the Latinized form of his name, Nostradamus, and Edgar Cayce, "the sleeping prophet."

There is also a great deal of information available from many lesser-known individuals who in one way or another appear to have the same abilities as Nostradamus or Cayce, but are not as yet accepted because their predictions and pronouncements have not stood the test of time. Finally, new scientific evidence and discoveries are coming to light that may explain and confirm many prophecies.

Matthew 24:29-30-31 reads:

> As soon as the distress of those days has passed, the sun will be darkened, the moon will not give her light, the stars will fall from the sky, the celestial powers will be shaken. Then will appear in heaven the sign that heralds the Son of Man.

In one of the most quoted and studied readings by Edgar Cayce relating to this time, we find the following excerpt:

> As to the material changes that are to be as an omen, as a sign to those that this is shortly to come to pass—as has been given of old, the sun will be darkened and the earth shall be broken up in divers places—and then shall be proclaimed—through the spiritual interception in the hearts and minds and souls that have sought His way—that His STAR has appeared. . ." (*World Affairs*, 3976-15, 1934)

No one is sure about the methodology of Nostradamus for his work—nor of the source of the information. His *Prophecies* were first published in 1555 in the form of verses known as quatrains. His fame quickly spread throughout France. In her book *The Man Who Saw Tomorrow,* Erika Cheetham says, "Nostradamus is probably the only author who could claim that his work has never been out of print for over four hundred years, apart from the Bible. On the average, about thirty books, either editions of the *Prophecies,* or critical appreciations of them, have been published each century since his death."

There are many quatrains from the *Prophecies* that refer to comets and similar heavenly or celestial bodies. The following are two examples from Cheetham's translation of the quatrains:

> After great misery for mankind an even greater
> approaches when the great cycle of the centuries
> is renewed. It will rain blood, milk, famine, war
> and disease: In the sky will be seen a fire,
> dragging a trail of sparks. (II-46)

> Mabus will then soon die and there will come a
> dreadful destruction of people and animals.
> Suddenly vengeance will be revealed, a hundred
> hands, thirst and hunger, when the COMET will
> pass. (II-62)

It can be argued, and justifiably so, that the interpretation of the quatrains, including the time placement of the predicted events, is difficult. However, since the accuracy of many has been established, the challenge to ascertain if others apply to future events that affect everyone on earth is irresistible to many. For instance, not long ago, most Nostradamus researchers pointed to Halley's comet as the likely fulfillment of these and similar quatrains. The word *Mabus* in quatrain II 62 is also a mystery. Many speculate that it is the proper name of a future leader, and point to the well-documented prophecies about "Hister," a type of anagram used by Nostradamus for Hitler. Cheetham states that Nostradamus wrote in an "obscure style" and that "in order to avoid being prosecuted as a magician, Nostradamus writes that he deliberately confused the time sequence of the *Prophecies* so that their secrets would not be revealed to the non-initiate."

(I've speculatedt about the term *Mabus* in the quatrain. There are lots of "experts" continually attempting to clarify the words and meaning of the quatrains. Some claim that Mabus is the name of a future, powerful world tyrant. Now I'm no expert (nor am I an initiate!) But if one substitutes the letter *M* with *N* and *B* with *D* you have *Nadus.* Then reverse the order, and we have *Sudan—a* country in Africa. We know currently the events on the continent of Africa, and the Republic of the Sudan. Now to continue along this line of thought, the proper name *Sudan* is from the French *Soudan,* and defined as "a region lying across Africa, south of the Sahara and north of the equator"—an area much greater than that of the country of Sudan. Was Nostradamus referring to the continent of Africa with this anagram? Who knows! Just an illustration of the problems evident with all predictions. Replace *Mabus* with *Africa* and see if somehow it fits. Now to continue with our ambiguous planet!)

For those who are interested in information, knowledge, theory, and more specifically prophecy that seems to manifest from a higher or unknown source, undoubtedly, other than the prophets of the Bible, Edgar Cayce and Nostradamus are the best known. However, many other lesser known gifted persons have demonstrated the same ability.

The work of one of these, Oscar Ernst Bernhardt, is published and distributed in more than a dozen countries. Designated the "Grail Message," it has already been useful to us in this discussion. It is composed of three large volumes entitled *In The Light of Truth,* authored under the pseudonym Abd-ru-shin.

The following, offered in the 1930s, is the complete text of his lecture on the subject of this dissertation:

The Great Comet

For years now *knowing ones* have been speaking of the coming of this especially significant STAR. The number of those who await it is continually increasing, and the indications become more and more definite, so much so in fact it is to be expected soon. But *what* it really signifies, what it brings, has not yet been rightly explained.

It is thought that it brings upheavals of an incisive nature. But this STAR portends more.

It can be called the Star of Bethlehem, because it is of exactly the same nature as that was. Its power sucks the *waters up high,* brings *weather catastrophes* and still more. When encircled by its rays the *earth quakes.*

Since the event in Bethlehem there has been nothing like it. Like the Star of Bethlehem, the STAR has also detached itself from the Eternal Realm of Primordial Spirit at such a time as to take effect on this earth exactly when the years of spiritual enlightenment are to come to all mankind.

The STAR takes its course in a *straight* line from the Eternal Realm of this part of the Universe. Its core is filled with high spiritual power; it envelopes itself in material substance, and will thereby also become visible to men on earth. Unerringly and unswervingly the COMET pursues its course, and will appear on the scene at the right hour, as already ordained thousands of years ago.

The first direct effects have already begun in recent years. For anyone who wishes neither to see nor to hear this, and who does not perceive how ridiculous it is still to maintain that all the *extraordinary* things which have already happened are of everyday occurrence, there is naturally no help. He either wishes to act like an ostrich out of fear, or he is burdened with an extremely limited understanding. Both types must be allowed to go serenely on their way; one can only smile at their easily refutable assertions.

But the knowing ones could also be told where the first *powerful* rays are striking. However, since the rays are gradually also encompassing the whole earth, there is no use being more explicit. It will take years to come to this point, and years before the COMET again releases the earth from its influence.

And then the earth is *purified* and *refreshed* in *every respect* for the blessing and joy of its inhabitants. It will be more beautiful than it has ever been. Therefore every believer shall look forward to the future with tranquil confidence, and not be alarmed at anything that may happen in the coming years. If he can look up with confidence to God no harm will come to him.

Now to present some recent scientific information, the purpose of which is to speculate on the possibility that this comet has been discovered, and that its appearance during this time will explain much that has heretofor remained an enigma.

Enter Zecharia Sitchin and the Twelfth Planet. Also referred to interchangeably by various sources as the Tenth Planet or Planet X.

Zecharia Sitchin was born in Russia and raised in Palestine, where he acquired a profound knowledge of modern and ancient Hebrew, other Semitic and European languages, the Old Testament, and the history and archaeology of the Near East. A graduate of the University of London, he was a leading journalist and editor in Israel for many years.

One of the few scholars able to read and understand Sumerian, he is the author of six books dealing with Earth's and man's histories and prehistories, on the information and texts written down on clay. If Sitchin's theories are true, the genie is released from the bottle. The key to a great riddle of our time has been discovered.

Because of the vast magnitude of the data and information in all his works, including his theories and conclusions, material from a recent book, *Genesis Revisited*, is our main reference for that presented here. Even then, it is very condensed and mainly pertains to matters that have possible scientific credibility, realizing that interested persons will want to investigate and reason further, and judge for themselves.

In January of 1981, the headline in The Detroit *News* read: "10th planet? Pluto's orbit says 'yes.'" It went on to report that an astronomer from the U.S. Naval Observatory "told a meeting of the American Astronomical Society. . .that irregularities in the orbit of Pluto. . .indicates that the solar system contains a 10th planet." It went on to explain that Pluto was discovered in 1930, not by observing it, but mathematically, from "the bulges that Pluto's gravitational field causes in the elliptical orbit of its closet neighbor, Neptune." (Interestingly, Pluto's orbit is so irregular or "perturbed" that it is briefly closer to the sun than that of Neptune.) It further reports this "announcement comes as no surprise to Zecharia Sitchin, whose book, *The 12th Planet*, came out three years ago."

As an aside, prior to the discovery of Pluto in 1930, the Cayce readings made mention of a planet he called "Septimus," which is the Latin word for seventh; Pluto being the seventh planet outward from (and including) the earth. Reading 826-8 categorically states that Pluto and the legendary "Vulcan" were one and the same.

More than eight years later, Sitchin again put his reputation on the line. NASA had launched Voyager 1 and Voyager 2. They were originally intended to reach and scan only Jupiter and Saturn. But scientists at NASA took advantage of a rare alignment of the outer planets and, using the gravitational forces of these planets as "slingshots," managed to thrust Voyager 2 first from Saturn to Uranus, and then from Uranus to Neptune. (Again, we are reminded that Neptune was discovered in 1846, after perturbations in the orbit of the somewhat nearer planet Uranus indicated the existence of another celestial body beyond it.) In August 1989, the dazzling images of the aquamarine Neptune appeared on television. It was repeatedly emphasized that this was the first time Man on Earth had ever been able to see this planet. It had been visible only by our best telescopes, as a dimly lit spot three billion miles from earth. However, two months before, relying on his intensive study of the Sumerian texts, Sitchin published several articles describing Neptune. He described it as "blue-green, watery" with "patches of swamplike vegetation," exactly what NASA found.

As interest in the media and the scientific world increased, Sitchin's theories and conclusions became more plausible. Perhaps the hard work and dedication of the past thirty years were coming to fruition.

In 1982 the U.S. Naval Laboratory announced that it was "seriously pursuing" the search for Planet X. In 1983 The New York *Times* reported: "Clues Get Warm in the Search for Planet X," and quoted an astronomer from the Ames Research Center as saying, "Astronomers are so sure of the 10th Planet that they think there's nothing left but to name it."

Of course, Sitchin already knew the name. To the Sumerians it was known as Nibiru, and to the Babylonians as Marduk.

Other reports appeared in several dailies:

Giant Object Mystifies Astronomers

Mystery Body Found in Space

At Solar System's Edge Giant Object is a Mystery

And so a debate arose, and a new dimension! For "reliable" sources had begun to speculate, and for good reason. These articles were based on an exclusive interview by Thomas O'Toole of the science service of The Washington *Post,* based on Infrared Astronomical Satellite (IRAS) data from the Pioneer spacecraft. The significant excerpt:

> Astronomers do not know if it is a planet or a giant comet. . .When IRAS scientists first saw the mystery body and calculated that it could be as close as 50 billion miles, there was some speculation that it might be moving toward earth.

The search and interest among scientists intensified. More reports appeared in the media. Sitchin wrote:

> By 1985 numerous astronomers were intrigued with the "Nemesis Theory" first proposed by Walter Alvarez of the University of California and his father, the Nobel-prize-winning physicist Luis Alvarez. Noticing the regularity in the extinctions of species of Earth (including the dinosaurs), they proposed that a "death star" or planet with a highly inclined and immense elliptical orbit periodically stirs up a shower of comets that then brings death and havoc to the inner Solar System, including Earth."

But could there be another reason for this "extinction"?

Edgar Cayce was asked the following question more than fifty years ago: What great change or the beginning of what change, if any, is to take place in the Earth in the year 2000 to 2001 A.D?" He answered, "When there is a shifting of the poles. Or a new cycle begins." (826-8)

In another reading about prehistoric times, Cayce discussed the "enormous animals which overran the Earth, but ice. . .nature, God, changed the poles, and the animals were destroyed." (5249-1) Also, concerning the "worlds existence" he says:

> . . .in the changes that have come in the Earth's plane. . .many lands have disappeared, many have appeared

and disappeared again and again. . .gradually changing as the condition became to the relative position of the earth with other spheres through which man passes in this solar system." (5748-2)

So now the size and scope of the Nemesis Theory expands dramatically. For if Sitchin's theories are correct, Planet X is headed our way.

In *The Twelfth Planet,* Sitchin says, "The Planet's periodic appearance and disappearance from Earth's view confirms the assumption of its permanence in solar orbit. In this it acts like many comets."

Sitchin claims that Planet X is about the size of Neptune, so, again, it was no surprise to him when, in August 1988, a report by Dr. Robert S. Harrington, of the U.S. Naval Laboratory calculated that "its mass. . .is probably four times that of Earth."

If these prophesies are accurate, the ramifications of Planet X entering our solar system would be hard to handle. If Planet X actually becomes visible to the naked eye—well, who can say? But one thing is certain: there will be speculation concerning the Second Coming of Jesus.

And in that regard, it is most interesting to note that Sitchin's research shows that the Sumerians assigned symbols to the heavenly bodies. And as the pictures depict on their clay tablets, along with their literature, the symbol for Marduk, Planet X, was the cross, with equal horizontal and vertical arms. This representation, of course, is a popular design that we often see today. No doubt, this would explain the Bible reference to "Then will appear in heaven the sign of the Son of Man," or from Cayce, "Then will be proclaimed. . .that His STAR has appeared." Also, in his earlier quoted poem, was Thomas Sugrue referring to the same celestial phenomena when he stated ". . .When the 20th Century shall have passed away and the *sign* of the God-man [Jesus?] is in the sky. . ."?

And what about the following reference from the same chapter of Matthew (of which similar verses also appear in one way or another throughout the Bible; best known in Luke and Revelations): "The sun will be darkened, the moon will not give her light, the stars will fall from the sky, the celestial powers will be shaken." And from the Cayce readings, paraphrasing the same chapter: "the sun will be darkened and the earth shall be broken up in divers places." And of course, we find similar pronouncements in the Nostradamus Quatrains, plus the prophecies of many, many other individuals and peoples. For if a comet the size of Planet X enters the Asteroid Belt between Mars and Jupiter, and in a retrograde orbit, as Sitchin claims, our solar system might be more than just a little stirred up. Add to this the effects of its gravitational pull on the earth, which would obviously cause earthquakes and strange weather patterns, and a possible Pole Shift, and the many "star"—"comet"—"fire from the sky" prophecies take on new meaning.

The existence of Planet X has not been proven, but evidence shows that it is very possible that the prospect of a tenth planet in our solar system may be proven in the near future. If this planet is discovered, who knows what ramifications it may bring? A second Ice Age? The Second Coming? One can only speculate and create a personal theory until, as with most things in science, it is proven, dismissed, or "still out there."

As you know, it wasn't long after we researched this material that other information on the same subject started coming to my attention. The first was from a reading offered by a well documented psychic living in Great Britain in the late 1970s. The following excerpt is from a reading titled: "The End of the World?"

> I must begin by emphasizing that there is a question mark after the title of this talk. I have not deliberately chosen this title in order to be provocative but merely to reflect the viewpoint of many people in your World today. Even amongst spiritually-minded people there are those who question the reason for the events now taking place on this planet, who ask whether the earth can survive, whether it should survive, who ask whether the Earth-changes to come are something to be avoided or welcomed. All I want to do in this talk is to present a point of view from another plane of life and to ask to hold it in your minds in the years to come.

> I will begin by making the simple statement that the

Earth, like you, is imbued with spirit. It will, therefore, never die. Whilst its physical form might change as it experiences periods of transformation and transmutation, the spirit that is responsible for its creation will never die. In the same way that you in your physical bodies die and are born again onto a higher plane of life so the Earth, on another level, undergoes a similar experience. It is a cosmic fact that all forms of life, no matter what the level of evolution, are born, die and are born again in the endless cycle of evolution. The Earth has done this many times, obviously not as frequently as you reincarnate in your physical bodies, and it will doubtless do this again.

Those of you on the plane of Earth who fear death, who do not understand the real nature of this act of transformation, will also fear the ending of the World because the result is apparently the same: the ending of physical life as you know it.

But those of you who are aware of life beyond death, who recognize that death on the plane of Earth is but the opening of a door to a higher level of consciousness, a return to the place of your true being, must also see that the same is true for the Earth as a whole. . .

The changes of which we talk now are the Earth-changes that are associated with the introduction of the Aquarian Age. It is essential that you who live at this time of transition should understand the nature of and the purpose for these Earth changes. . .

Remember that the symbol of the Aquarian Age is the "phoenix." The phoenix is the mythical bird which consciously sacrifices itself on the cosmic fire, releasing its old form in order to come forth purified in the new. Does not the phoenix symbolize the desire within your own spiritual being for the purification of the Earth to take place so that the old human form can be cast off and the new Aquarian form may come forth? As you look around the World today you cannot help but notice the increasing tempo of human conflict all over the globe as both nations and individuals oppose each other for political, ideological, and religious reasons. But humanity is not only suffering from an outer level through famine, earthquake, disease and war but also on an inner level through its lack of spirituality, its self-centeredness, its greed, its concern only for self at the expense of its fellow human beings and the other Kingdoms of the Earth. All these events bear witness to the approach of Armageddon and the ending of the Age. Humanity needs to be purified. Humanity needs to experience the cosmic fire of purification in order to come forth reborn in the Aquarian Age.

I know there are some people, some spiritually motivated, who believe that this event will not come about and that it will be prevented either by the intervention of some great Master or by Humanity reversing the path upon which it is now set. I would ask you to remember the impact of the last great impulse of the Christ energy, of the Master Jesus who came on the Earth two thousand years ago. Consider how long it took for that energy to become an effective force on the plane of Earth even after that Master's great sacrifice. Even if the Christ energy was to return at this time it could not move Humanity from the course on which it set. That is why the prophets and seers of old could make their prophecies with such certainty. To ground cosmic knowledge on the Earth, to manifest it through the cycle of human evolution, takes time, human time. The spiritual consciousness needed to save this World cannot be grounded in the time that is now left before the Earth-changes.

Those of you who recognize this fact, not knowing when this great moment of transformation will come about but trusting only that it will be a divine act, inspired by Divine will, might ask what is the purpose of your being. As I have said in the past, the analogy of a lifeboat should come to mind. You sail on the great ship of Mother Earth. At present you are sailing in calm waters, for you are living in the rosy days of Western Civilization. . .you have the best of this Earth.

See yourselves, therefore, as lifeboats of consciousness, as lifeboats designed not for this moment in time but for the storms to come. If I may use an analogy, you are the Noahs of the last great cataclysm. You are receiving your divine inspiration to build your arks, not arks of physical matter but arks of spiritual consciousness, consciousness to understand the Earth-changes that will come, consciousness to understand the death and destruction that must inevitably follow and, above all, consciousness to rebuild human civilization and to ensure its continuing growth in the future. This Age will see the physical manifestation of the divine principles which you now hold only as ideals, as spiritual concepts in your innermost soul beings. Everything of the highest that you wish was upon Earth will be grounded upon her. All things will be possible in the New Age.

How, and when, are these Earth-changes to come about? They can come about in several ways depending on whether they are initiated by human destruction or by divine intervention. As to the timing of this event there are many opinions but, in truth, there is only one being who possess that knowledge and that is your God, the Creator of us all. Furthermore that knowledge will not be released to anyone until the actual moment in time draws near.

I believe that the major Earth-changes will be initiated by what I will call the "Fiery Messenger." There is even now a star of great power proceeding towards our Solar Body. The star, at this moment, is invisible to the human, or even telescopic eye, but it is set on a path which will bring it into conjunction with our Planetary System. As it passes by it will affect the motions of all the planets of our System, therefore, will bring about changes on the surface of the planets themselves. The effect of the passage will be to set in motion the Earth-changes that are prophesied. Various lands will sink, others will rise. . .

Humanity has the power to influence the nature of this transformation through its behavior now, through its use of nuclear technology, through its use, or abuse, of the three Kingdoms of Matter on this Earth. It can either add to, or moderate, the path and the influence of this great star. How you as individuals behave now, how you lead your lives and manifest your consciousness will affect the great transformation of the Earth. So I say to you now, as I said to you five years ago, that these Earth-changes are coming. They cannot be avoided. They are part of the destiny of the Earth.

Is it not strange how Humanity finds it difficult to plan beyond the year 2000. It is almost as if the end of the century is the ending of a cycle. Now I'm not saying that this is the year when these changes will come to pass, but certainly the final ending of the Piscean cycle will indeed take place around that time. This therefore gives you two decades in which to prepare yourselves, to prepare your lifeboats, to establish your true values, to shine your light and to prepare for the ending of your world. I hasten to say *your* world, not *the* World, for it is your world that must change, not the World. . .The divinity of planet Earth will not be extinguished by any human action. . .

Although Humanity has the power to destroy itself, it will destroy itself not by nuclear explosions, not by destroying the planet which it abuses out of ignorance and greed, *but by destroying its own soul.*

Question: The star that was spoken of, has it passed through this Solar System before?

Answer: Yes.

Question: Is it Halley's comet?

Answer: No. It is far bigger than that.

Shortly after I discovered this information, I found the following prophecy by the German seer, St. Hildegarde, concerning "the comet" as quoted in the book *Rolling Thunder, The Coming Earth Changes,* by J.R. Jochmans.

A Twelfth Century Prophecy About America

Perhaps the earliest vision ever made concerning the future of the United States was made by Saint Hildegarde, three centuries before the New World was discovered. She predicted that one day there would come forth "a great nation across the ocean that will be inhabited by peoples of different tribes and descent"—a good description of the American "melting pot" of immigrants from many foreign countries. For this future nation, however, the Saint sounded several warnings, all of which would come about near or at the time of the appearance of a "great comet." Some translators believe what she had in mind was Halley's comet, scheduled to light up our heavens in 1986-87.

"Just before the comet comes," Saint Hildegarde forecast, "many nations" including America, "will be scourged by want of famine." When the comet does finally pass over. . ."the great nation will be devastated by earthquakes, storms, and great waves of water, causing much want and plagues. The ocean will also flood many other countries, so that all coastal cities will live in fear, with many destroyed. . ."

Fortunately, however, Saint Hildegarde looked beyond, and also forecast that after the great comet, and after earth upheavals and wars are finished, the globe will eventually enter a peaceful age.

It will be a time when citizens of the "great nation" will carry no weapons, and the only use men will have for iron will be to make plowshares for cultivating a land brought back to abundance and tranquility.

There are hundreds of prophecies attributed to church clergy, saints, and seers. Many mention cosmic disturbances and turmoil of numerous descriptions. For example, the following quote is from *Prophecies and Predictions*, Moira Timms' first book:

Johann Friede (1204-1257), an Austrian monk of the order of St. John, was one of the greatest seers of his time. An excerpt from one of his many revelations follows: "When the great time will come, in which mankind will face its last, hard trial, it will be foreshadowed by striking changes in nature. The alteration between cold and heat will become more intensive, storms will have more catastrophic effects, earthquakes will destroy greater regions and the seas will overflow many lowlands. Not all of it will be the result of natural causes, but mankind will penetrate into the bowels of the earth and will reach into the clouds, gambling with its own existence. Before the powers of destruction will succeed in their design, the universe will be thrown into disorder, and the age of iron will plunge into nothingness.

"When nights will be filled with more intensive cold and days with heat, a new life will begin in nature. The heat means radiation from the earth, the cold the waning light of the sun. Only a few years more and you will become aware that sunlight has grown perceptibly weaker. When even your artificial light will cease to give service, the great event in the firmament [heavens] will be near. . ."

It's interesting that this prophecy refers to "the age of iron." A friend, David Solomon, refers to the following in an unpublished article he wrote:

According to Hindu tradition of cosmology, we are now nearing the end of the "Kali Yuga"—"the Age of Iron."

We read in the *Visuddi-Magga,* a book from ancient India: ". . .there are seven ages, each of which is separated from the previous one by a world catastrophe." According to Mahabharata from ancient India we are presently living in Kali Yuga, "the Age of Destruction" which is described as follows:

"When men begin to slay one another, and become wicked and fierce and without any respect for animal life, then will Yuga come to an end. . .And when flowers will be begot within flowers and within fruits [hybrid seeds, genetic engineering?] then will the Yuga come to an end."

The *Vishnu Purana,* one of the oldest sacred texts of India says about Kali Yuga, "The leaders who rule over the earth will be violent and seize the goods of their subjects. . .The leaders, with the excuses of fiscal need, will rob and despoil their subjects and take away private property. Moral values and the rule of law will lessen from day to day until the world will be completely perverted and agnosticism will gain the day among men."

Conjecture, speculation: is it a comet or a star, or the invention of over-active imaginations? So many thousands of years of legends about sightings and happenings repeating at certain intervals.

From *Doomsday 1999 A.D.* by language expert Charles Berlitz is the following concerning the ancient prophecies of the Hopi Indians:

The Hopi, a small Amerindian tribe of very ancient tradition, apparently knew that the earth turned on its axis. In a Hopi legend the axis of the earth was guarded by a pair of cosmic giants who, when they left their positions, caused the earth to falter in its spin. . .and the start of a new era. The beginning of the end of the present or "Fourth World" is considered by the Hopi to have already started·and will be consummated after the appearance of a now invisible star, rushing towards Earth from space.

From David Solomon:

The Celestial Lord Shiva, God of destruction, was known to ancient peoples as a vast, fiery body, that when it entered the solar system, caused planetary catastrophes. . .Of this apparition, Pliney wrote "A terrible comet was seen by the people of Ethiopia and Egypt, to which the name Typhon, the king of the period, gave his name; it had a fiery appearance and was twisted like a coil; and it was grim to behold. And Heavenly fire is spit forth by this planet as crackling flies from a burning log."

The celestial Body was known to the Latins as Lucifer, to the ancient Greeks as Typhon, to the Mayans as Celestial Quetzalcoatl, to the ancient Sumerians as Nibiru (Planet of the Crossing), to the ancient Chinese as Gung-gung, the Great Black or Red Dragon, to the Phoenicians as the Great Phoenix, to the ancient Hebrews as Yahweh, and to the ancient Egyptians as Apep, or Seth.

Over two thousand years ago, Solon [a Greek statesman and philosopher credited with being the founder of democracy] visited Egypt to exchange information concerning history and genealogies. One of the High Priests told him: "Solon, you are young in soul, every one of you. For therein you possess not a single science that is hoary with age. And this is the cause thereof—there have been and there will be many diverse destructions of mankind, of which the greatest are by fire and water, and lesser ones by countless other means. . .but the truth of it lies in the occurrence of a shifting of the bodies in the heavens which surround the earth, and destruction of the things on earth by fierce fire, like a plague, the flood from heaven comes sweeping down afresh upon your people, it leaves none of you but the unlettered and the uncultured, so that you become young as ever, with no knowledge of all that happened in old times in this land or in your own. Certainly the genealogies which you related just now, Solon, concerning the people of your country, are little better than children's tales; for in the first place, you remember but one deluge, though many have occurred previously."

From what I can surmise concerning the comet/star, almost every single source claims that the phenomenon is a recurring event! The only differences seem to be in the interval of time; however, the majority put the interval at 30,000 years or less. The most popular estimate is 3600 years, which would place its most recent appearance during the time of the Exodus as described in the Old Testament, and at the time of Noah before that. And of course, if you want to accept the one-time existence of Atlantis as characterized by Plato and so many others, it also had something to do with the destruction of Atlantis.

Concerning the time of the Exodus, the following is excerpted and paraphrased from *Catholic Prophecy, The Coming Chastisement* by Yves Dupont, discussing the return of the comet:

Let us recall briefly the situation which afflicted the Egyptians, the crossing dry-shod of the Red Sea and the prolonged duration of the day. In Mexico, on the other hand, a prolonged night was recorded, as evidenced by archaeological discoveries. The passage of the comet at that time was recorded, not only in the book of Exodus, but also in other documents: the Egyptian papyrus, a Mexican manuscript, a Finnish narration, and many others. . .

Will the comet to come be the same as that of Exodus? It is not impossible when we consider the description of the plagues as given in Exodus and those described in our Christian prophecies. When the tail of the Exodus comet crossed the path of the earth, a red dust, impalpable, like fine flour, began to fall. It was too fine to be seen. . .but it colored everything red and the water of the Egyptians was changed into blood. . . After the fine rusty pigment fell over Egypt, there followed a coarser dust—"like ash," this is recorded in Exodus, for then it was visible. . .

The narrative of the Book of Exodus confirms this and

168

is in turn corroborated by various documents found in Mexico, Finland, Siberia, and India. It is therefore certain that a comet crossed the path of the earth more than 3000 years ago, causing widespread destruction. This is the kind of phenomenon (if the prophecies are accurate) which is soon to strike the earth again.

If it is a "repeat" event, and if the time intervals are equal, then that would in part explain why so many seers could predict the birth pangs of the New Age with confidence.

The "Grail Message" counsels: "Men! When the hour comes in which, according to the Divine Will, the purification and winnowing must take place on earth, then watch for the predicted and partly supernatural signs in the sky!"

Mother Shipton, who lived in England during the 1500s, is said to have been one of the most accurate seers of her time. She had an unusual ability to predict events in other countries, such as the U.S.A. and Australia. She even described the use of products not yet known to Europe, such as potatoes and tobacco. She wrote in rhyming verses, of which the following are a few examples that seem to point to the present time:

> Carriages without horses shall go,
> And accidents fill the world with woe.
> Around the earth thoughts shall fly,
> In the twinkling of an eye.
> Through hills men shall ride,
> And no horse be at his side.
> Under water men shall walk,
> Shall ride, shall sleep, shall talk.
> Iron in the water shall float,
> As easily as a wooden boat.
> Taxes for blood and war,
> Shall come to every door.
> When women dress like men and trousers wear,
> And cut off all their locks of hair.
> When pictures look alive with movements free,
> When ships like fishes swim beneath the sea,
> When men outstripping birds can soar the sky,
> Then half the world, deep drenched in blood,
> shall die. . .

Of course, as I mentioned earlier, there will be other signs or clues for humanity's edification—if one's interest is so inclined. There are many others that seem to fit the mold. For example, in the predictions there are many references to civil disturbances—racial problems—anarchy—and so forth during this period.

Could this be that decisive period some refer to as the Last Judgment? If so, is everyone ready and eager? Well, there are several theories concerning this subject.

The first is the Either—Or Theory, and the following are some examples regarding it.

This reading was offered in the early 1980s from the same psychic from England who predicted the "fiery messenger" earlier quoted:

> . . .follow that inner light and be true to it. I can reassure you that there is a Plan for this Earth, that there is a great Being overseeing that Plan and that no evil thing can touch you if you are but true to yourself. Though many may suffer around you, though many may perish, though there may be droughts and floods, earthquakes and cataclysms, those who are true to that Spirit within will survive, and by survive I do not necessarily mean the survival of the *physical body but the survival of the Spirit* [soul] on the higher planes of life. For the Day of Judgment is coming, the time when the wheat must be sorted from the chaff if this planetary system is to move upward on the evolutionary spiral. Now that does not mean that those who are not chosen are faced with extermination. It merely means that they will return to what could be called a *Group Energy* and will allow those who have earned the right to individuality, [that "aware individual" again] who have recognized the Divinity of their being, to progress further along their evolutionary paths and so fulfil their potential.

The "Grail Message" also declares this to be the time of the Either-Or and points to this time as the period of the great evolution for all that began in the 1930s.

Another scenario is the Held-Out Theory. Is the New Age reserved for those souls who, having decided by acting in accord with God's will, shall be the only ones allowed to incarnate in the earth during the "thousand years of peace" described in the Bible? From the book of Revelation, 20:1-6:

> Then I saw an angel coming down from heaven with the key of the abyss and a great chain in his hands. He seized the dragon, that serpent of old, the Devil or Satan, and chained him up for a thousand years; he threw him into the abyss, shutting and sealing it over him, so that he might seduce the nations no more till the thousand years were over. . .then those who had not worshiped the beast. . .came to life again and reigned with Christ for a thousand years, though the rest of the dead did not come to life until the thousand years were over. This is the first resurrection. . . happy indeed. . .is the man who shares in the first resurrection!

Edgar Cayce gave many readings on the Book of Revelation. With regards to these passages he was asked:

> Q: What is the meaning of the thousand years that Satan is bound?
> A: Is banished. That. . .in the same manner that the prayer of ten just [persons] should save a city, the deeds, the prayers of the faithful will allow that period when the incarnation of those only that are in the Lord shall rule the earth, and the period is a thousand years.
> Thus is Satan bound, thus is Satan banished from the earth. The desire to do evil is only of him. And when there are—as the symbols—those only whose desire and purpose of their heart is to glorify the Father, these will be those periods when this shall come to pass. Be ye ALL DETER-MINED within thy minds, thy hearts, thy purposes, to be of that number. (281-37)

What about the souls that are "held out" for the thousand years? What's going on "over there" during this period? Is the Saturn hotel the only one open for business? Are souls that incarnate on planet earth going to live one lifetime for a thousand years?

In his book *Why Jesus Taught Reincarnation*, ordained mini-ster, clinical psychologist, and Cayce researcher Herbert Bruce

Puryear explains his interpretation as follows:

> During the thousand years of peace, Satan will be bound, that is, no souls who are still rebellious will be permitted to incarnate. . .Those [who are] incarnate during the thousand years of peace, under the leadership of the Master, will have prepared a most promising environment into which the others may reenter [the souls that were vacationing on Saturn—the "rest of the dead"?—now have another opportunity to incarnate]. . .The purpose of the Millennium is to establish a planetary classroom of the greatest strength and purity in order to continue the ongoing work of the plan of salvation of all of God's children who are entrapped in this system. . .The reincarnation view makes sense of it all. . .

The following passage from Yves Dupont seems to fit the Held-Out Theory:

> Christ Himself has warned us that "no one knows of the day and hour, not even the angels of heaven, but the Father only". . . Christ gave us a number of signs to watch for. . .(1) The Gospel shall be preached in the whole world, (2) A universal falling away from the faith, (3) The coming of Antichrist, (4) The return of the Jews to the Holy Land, and (5) Widespread disturbances of nature. . ."the powers of heaven shall be shaken. . .the stars shall fall from heaven. . .widespread earthquakes, tidal waves, lightning, wars, famines, and epidemics shall occur."
>
> Now, the question is this: Have any of these signs come to pass already? [This was published in 1970.] The answer cannot be definite and clear cut. It may be asserted that the first two signs are already here: indeed the Gospel has been preached in every nation, and there is overwhelming evidence of a general falling away from the Faith. Yet, it has been, and it may still be contended that the preaching of the Gospel must be absolutely world-wide and reach every single human being, and not merely confined to pockets of missionary activity in every nation. It can also be objected that the current faithlessness is not general enough to be applied to the second sign. . .

In my opinion. . .there are two different stages within the "Latter-Days" period; the first. . .being of lesser intensity, the final stage bringing about the consummation of the world. To each of these two stages will the proximate signs of the "End" apply. Thus we are about to enter the first stage, the "Great Disaster" which is imminent and which will be followed by a period of peace.

This personal interpretation of mine is based on my knowledge of a large number of private prophecies, and on extensive and painstaking cross-references and correlations made many years ago. . .moreover, this interpretation is not incompatible with Scripture. Indeed, Scripture supports it in many cases. We read in the Gospel, for instance, a description of various evils followed by the caution: "But the End is not yet." (Matthew 24:6), and again the descriptions of pestilence, famines and earthquakes, with the conclusion: "But these are the beginnings of sorrows" (Matt 24:8), the first stage only. Then we are told that "the Gospel will be preached in the whole world" (Matthew 24:14) before the End finally comes.

Is it possible the answer is "none of the above?"

There is one Cayce reading that is unusual and difficult to interpret. It was given in December 1943, about one year before Cayce's death, for a ten-year-old boy. The following is an excerpt:

Let that rather be thy watchword, "I am my brothers keeper"...Who is thy brother? All that are in the earth today are thy brothers. *Those that have gradually forgotten God entirely have been eliminated,* and there has come—now—and will come at the close of this next year—the period when there will be no part of the globe where man has not had the opportunity to hear, "The Lord God He is God."

And, as has been indicated, when this period has been accomplished, then the new era, the New Age, is to begin. Will ye have a part of it, or will ye let it pass by and just be a *hanger-on. . .?*

This reading is hard to interpret. It seems to best fit into the Held-Out Theory, but I'm not sure. Maybe someone will enlighten us! In the meantime, I don't think it is such a good idea to let the New Age "pass by"—it could be risky. What would I be "hanging on" to—could it be one of those rings that surround the planet Saturn?

Who Was That Masked Man?

When I was a young boy, we didn't have television. But we did have the radio and our imagination. There were several adventure programs, known as serials, that were broadcast after school let out. My friends and I would listen to three or four of these almost every afternoon.

One of the most popular was "The Lone Ranger," which, as you are aware, eventually became a television series.

At the end of every episode, without fail, after the Lone Ranger and his faithful Indian companion Tonto had solved a mystery, righted a wrong, or saved a maiden's life, they would ride off into the sunset as the Lone Ranger urged his horse Silver into a gallop.

Then came the question from one of the bystanders or eyewitnesses—"Who was that masked man?"

Every once in a while a similar question comes to my mind when exploring all of the ramifications, the good elements and the bad ones, of psychic or extrasensory information—now mostly referred to as "channeling." Who was (or is) that masked entity or spirit or something? To what frequency is the psychic antenna being tuned? What station? What program is being broadcast? Is there static interference during the transmission? Who is the announcer? Is there more than one announcer at the ethereal microphone? Who decides the advice program that will be listened to? Why is the announcer-guide's name very often a mysterious or ancient one; is it intended to invoke awe and respect? Is this a scheme designed to add credibility to the masked entity— communication with a higher power or intelligence? Are there not any guides named George or Harry— Nancy or Flo?

These are the type of questions everyone should ask. For the *source* of this type of information is the most important consideration in determining the validity of the statements, advice, and remarks offered in the communication.

In the talk by Edgar Cayce that I quoted early on in this correspondence, he says: "As a matter of fact, it would seem to be not just one, but several sources of information tapped when I am in this sleeping state. . .As to the validity of the information that comes through me, this is the question, naturally, that occurs to everyone."

To once again quote his son, Edgar Evans Cayce:

> Some have the mistaken idea that all Cayce readings have the same validity, that suggestions for a particular individual have universal application and that everything Cayce said about any subject is true. Nothing could be farther from the truth. My brother and I spent much time compiling a book, *The Outer Limits Of Edgar Cayce's Power,* which deals specifically with the problem of readings that seemed to have been wrong and why this was so. I am sure he [Hugh Lynn Cayce, who passed over in 1982] would join with me in recommending that anyone researching the Cayce readings read this book first, at least the chapter on "The Nature of Psychic Perception."

> It is true that many individuals received help, in some cases remarkable cures, from the Cayce physical readings. It is also true that some suggestions he made for certain ailments may have general application. On the TV program "Unsolved Mysteries" that featured a segment about Edgar Cayce, the case of a young woman with an extremely serious eye disease, optic neuritis, was dramatized. She was going blind. This woman never had a reading, but under medical supervision, she followed suggestions Cayce gave years ago for a similar problem and recovered.

> The claims Cayce made in life readings in the early 1920s and 1930s that conflicted with the accepted scientific knowledge; the ones that insisted human beings had been in North America and South America thousands of years before it was at that time believed, have been verified by recent discoveries and radio carbon dating techniques.

> It is a fact that some readings are better than others, more specific, give more detailed information. In researching the

readings for data for our book, Hugh Lynn and I found approximately 200 readings out of the more than 14,000 Cayce gave that seemed to be wrong. There may be others, though certainly the evidence is that the vast majority of the readings he gave were accurate.

There are most likely several possible sources for the information Cayce gave. A great many *factors* were all influential in directing Cayce to a particular source.

Thereupon, once contact with the source was accomplished, he had to interpret the data received, and translate it into intelligible words and sentences that formed the reading.

Some of the factors influencing the source contacted were:

1. Unconsciousness memory.

2. Clairvoyant memory.

3. Telepathic communication between Edgar Cayce's subconscious or superconscious mind and that of other individuals living or dead.

4. The manner in which his subconscious was directed by the conductor of the reading at its beginning largely determined where he made attunement.

5. The possibility that in his unconscious state, to Cayce, the past, present, and future existed at once and he was able to see events that had happened, that were happening, and an infinite number of possibilities of which *some were more probable than others*.

Some factors influencing the accuracy included:

1. Physical and emotional health of Edgar Cayce.

2. The source he contacted for specific information.

3. Attitudes, emotions, prejudices, and especially the *desires*, of the many individuals that in any way were involved with a particular reading.

It seems probable from these conclusions by Edgar Cayce's son, an experienced and proficient researcher of the readings, that trying to determine the source of a given reading, along with the accuracy, is not easy. A great deal of ongoing research is necessary to substantiate such an expanse of information. Certainly, much has been accomplished in researching and documenting the information, and a substantial amount of data, of the suggestions and pronouncements, have been confirmed to a greater or lesser degree. I feel the reliability of a vast majority of the Cayce readings will, in time, be proven out.

It is often stated that Edgar Cayce got his information from the Universal Mind. The use of this term seems to denote an all-knowing source that is never mistaken. Yet the term *universal* encompasses all that is in our world and the universe. And as we have seen demonstrated, there are many realms, and dimensions within realms, in the universe.

All human beings who claim a special gift of psychic ability attempt to reach out into one of these realms for information; or at least that is what they say they do. Some, however, are obtaining information from their own subconscious mind or that of another.

Regardless of the source, because the subconscious mind is the soul mind, it follows that, along with the other factors explained by Edgar Evans Cayce, the *spiritual development* of the soul of each person involved with a particular activity of a psychic nature affects the information obtained and the correctness of advice given.

When the psychic's subconscious mind reaches out into one of the realms, his spiritual soul development, as reflected in his soul's vibration, again determines the maximum vibrational altitude in which he can still breathe. In addition, the soul vibration of the person seeking the psychic information may restrict, or hold back, the altitude of the psychic. The same is true when the information is solely from the psychic's subconscious memory. Finally, on the other side there are souls or spirits who are not any smarter or any wiser then we are.

In 1933 a lady sought help from Edgar Cayce through a reading to "relieve her of difficulties she was having from hearing voices that mocked and frightened her." She heard these voices as whisperings close to her ear.

She had been experimenting with what is known as "automatic writing"—a very questionable routine, where one sits motionless at a table, with the conscious mind quieted, pen in hand resting on a sheet of paper, in order to receive messages from the other side. The voices she heard were at first helpful, giving answers to her questions and guidance regarding her daily problems. The ethereal spirits had baited the hook, and she had swallowed it, hook, line, and sinker. Gradually the voices began to criticize her thoughts and actions. Incorrect information was given, and finally frightening lies were whispered to her constantly, such as, "There is a snake in your room. It is under the bed and when you go to sleep it is going to crawl over you. —Your husband is seeing another woman.—Someone is peeping through the window at you." The preface to the reading states, "A trip to the doctor's office would be the first move toward an institution, so she turns to Edgar Cayce as her only hope."

The reading states, ". . .it would be well to consider the character of the source. . .The influences of forces from without are as those seen in the material world, *good* and *bad*. . ."

It appears this person had at least limited psychic ability that was difficult to control and couldn't be shut off at will. For she asked Cayce: "How can I discern the helpful entities or forces from those forces that would do me harm?" He answered:

> In each experience ask that they acknowledge the life, the death, the resurrection of the Jesus, the Christ. They that answer only as in the affirmative; otherwise, "Get thee behind me, I will have no part with thee. Through His name only will I accept direction!" (422-1)

In his book *Venture Inward,* in Part III, "Dangerous Doorways to the Unconscious," Hugh Lynn Cayce recounts several cases of the disastrous consequences that were inflicted upon individuals that started fooling around with automatic writing, and the just-as-dangerous Ouija board. The following excerpt is an example:

> The following story came from a young mechanic. He lived with his attractive wife (age 24) and two children (ages 4 and 6) in their own home in a suburb of a large western city. The husband read science fiction and some of the more sensational magazines in the psychic field.
>
> One day he brought home a Ouija board. A magazine article had suggested it as a possible means of communication with the dead. He and his wife began experiments with

the board and obtained messages purportedly from various entities who identified themselves as dead friends and members of the family. The couple got answers to their questions involving clairvoyance and telepathy. They appeared to be picking up the thoughts and actions of their neighbors. When confronted with the information, the neighbors expressed astonishment at the accuracy and details. The man and his wife used the board for entertainment and fun to astound and perplex their friends. The wife was told through the board that she was a "sensitive" and that she could do automatic writing. She sat with pad and pencil and soon was able to write rapidly in a legible hand, continuing apparently the same type information secured through the Ouija board.

One morning while washing dishes after her husband had gone to work, she heard a soft whisper just back of her left ear. The more she responded to the suggestion of this voice and the more she followed the information, the clearer it became. She was warned of accidents with the children and was told where she could find things she had lost.

After about ten days the soft voice changed to a hard one; the gentle whisper became a shrill scream. The woman was told that she was in "his" power; that she had been playing long enough.

The voice went on to identify himself as a discarnate entity who was in love with her. She was told that she did not belong to her husband. The entity claimed that he was going to kill her in order to bring her to "his plane." All food would sicken her and she would literally starve to death.

The woman maintained enough balance after this experience to call her husband. They were both convinced that she was probably going insane. The husband could now get no information in any attempts at writing, or if there were responses the voice brought only accusations, filthy language, and insistence that the wife would soon be dead. The woman related that to her horror she could not even drink water without vomiting. The couple went to a doctor who recommended a psychiatrist. They did not follow his suggestion, fearing the wife would be committed to an institution.

The woman tried fighting the voice, and at times it seemed to be quiet or remote. At such times she was able to take small quantities of liquid food and retain them. However, as soon as the voice reappeared, sometimes catching her in the act of eating, she would immediately be overcome with nausea. The horror persisted for days. Gradually she became aware of something she described as a psychic presence. The voice kept insisting that she would be able to feel and see him.

Unfortunately, the husband was transferred to an early shift at his plant. One morning he arose early, prepared his own breakfast, and left. In a few moments the woman was horrified as she became aware of a form in the bed with her. She was overcome with loathing and terror, yet was unable to prevent a sexual stimulation. . .Her husband arrived after an emergency call. They decided to give up the fight and go to a psychiatrist, recognizing that the family would probably be broken up and that she would be committed for treatment as insane. To their great relief, they were able to secure the cooperation of a physician who was willing to consider the psychic implications of this bizarre series of experiences. Prayer, physiotherapy, and work with a psychically gifted person were included in the treatment which enabled the couple to return to near normalcy.

There are many more similar and frightening stories of this type; not only in this book, but in lots of others.

The bottom line: don't mess around with the Ouija board or automatic writing. You can easily become hooked—and once the masked entity on the other side announces its true desires and starts reeling you into its boat, neither the Lone Ranger nor Tonto will be able to gallop across the ethereal water to your rescue.

This is simply another form of possession. There are a lot of ways to open up your protective energy body to unwelcome intruders from the beyond. And these deranged spirits are not interested in visiting your dwelling to hand you a birthday gift. They belong to the same ethereal gang that Dr. Ritchie described he saw in the lower realms surrounding the earth. What Cayce sometimes referred to as the "borderland."

In another example, Hugh Lynn quotes from correspondence

he had been receiving from a distraught woman who was plagued by evil spirits: ". . .they make us feel remorse or lack of it, hates and desires. Sex is an obsession with them, also food, drink, all forms of pleasure. These spirits were of the earth-earthy, I suppose, and have never progressed toward the spiritual development they must attain."

Another case history that Hugh Lynn describes is that of a lady who, by way of Ouija board, was told that "Emerson and Jesus were only two of the distinguished entities who claimed to be communicating." She had been specially "chosen" as an assistant to aid humanity with the help of their guidance. Her experiences with the board "brought her to the brink of a complete physical and nervous collapse."

There is today, instructional material based on psychic information, that is popular and studied by a large number of people, that certain researchers have questioned concerning the source being channeled, and the suggestions and counsel offered. The collection is titled *A Course In Miracles (ACIM)*.

The following is the full text from an article that appeared in the *Insight Newsletter* published by the Insight Foundation for ACIM, under the heading "Understanding the Crucifixion." The various numbers after ACIM quotes refer to the page of the text (T) or workbook (W) of the first and second editions. It was written by ACIM instructor John Harvey and are his ideas, personal interpretations, and understanding of some of the concepts found in the course. Here again, the question of *interpretation* and *source* must be considered. It is my understanding that most, if not all of the teachings in ACIM, are claimed to have come from Jesus himself. The psychic channel was a psychologist by the name of Helen Schucman.

"Jesus must have had attack thoughts in order to be crucified," a student of mine commented. "Because according to the Course, without attack thoughts nothing can hurt you. So maybe he wasn't as evolved as we were meant to believe."

"You're forming a very definite conclusion without considering both sides of the issue," I told her.

"What do you mean?"

"Well, there are actually two opposing premises to consider in the crucifixion issue," I said. "The two premises are that, either Jesus DID have attack thoughts, and therefore WAS crucified, or Jesus DID NOT have attack thoughts, and therefore not crucified."

"But the Bible says he WAS crucified," my student said.

"Right," I told her. "But have you noticed that Jesus refers to the Bible as 'the teachings of the Apostles.' (T 87/95) It was the Apostles who said that he was crucified. Jesus didn't say it. And according to Jesus, the Apostles DID have attack thoughts, because he says that they 'couldn't speak of the crucifixion entirely without anger.' (T 87/94)

"But what do THEIR attack thoughts have to do with HIS crucifixion?" my student asked.

"Let me explain," I said. "The course says that 'each of your perceptions of external reality is a pictorial representation of your attack thoughts.' (W 34/34) Therefore the crucifixion as perceived by the Apostles, in their own private worlds, was THEIR pictorial representation of THEIR OWN attack thoughts, and had nothing to do with Jesus."

"What?" my student exclaims. "The crucifixion had nothing to do with Jesus?"

"In His private world," I said, "Jesus was NOT crucified, precisely BECAUSE he had no attack thoughts. Jesus explains in the Course that each person has a 'private world that cannot be shared.' (T 230/247) Therefore, Jesus in his world, DID NOT share the crucifixion nightmare that the Apostles made in THEIR worlds."

"Is this what the Course says?" my student asked.

"Oh yes, many times. For example, Jesus says that 'the crucifixion cannot be shared.' (T 87/94) And he explains that he 'was persecuted as the world judges, and did not share this evaluation for myself.' (T 85/92) He also says 'you are not persecuted, nor was I.' (T 86/94) And then he says that 'the crucifixion had no part in it,' (T 264/284) clearly indicating that he took no part in the crucifixion, but only in the resurrection, which was his awakening."

"So you're saying that the Apostles 'mocked up' the

crucifixion in their own private worlds, but in his own private world Jesus was not crucified?"

"Exactly. What the Apostles perceived as Jesus in their own private worlds was NOT Jesus but a figure they made up which was their INTERPRETATION of Jesus. The Course says what you perceive is your interpretation."

"Jesus says 'again and again have you attacked your brother, because you saw in him a shadow figure in your private world. And thus it is you must attack yourself first, for what you attack is not in others.' (T 23/248) And so, what the Apostle saw as being crucified was actually an illusory figure which was a part of their own split mind, and not Jesus at all. In your madness you overlook reality completely, and you see only your own split mind everywhere you look. (T 231/248) No one can crucify anyone else! You can only crucify yourself, because you are the only one in your private world.

"For these figures have no witnesses, being perceived in one separate mind only. (T 231/248) Jesus says that "this world is a picture of the crucifixion of God's Son. And until you realize that God's Son cannot be crucified, this is the world you will see." (T 232/249)

"But in certain parts of the Course," my student said, "it appears as if Jesus is saying that he WAS crucified. For example, he says that 'you are not asked to be crucified, which was part of my own teaching contribution.'" (T 85/93)

"Right," I told her. "You see, Jesus has 'tuned in' to our private worlds in order to help us out of our illusions. He says, 'I am with them, as I am with you, and we will draw them from their private worlds.'" (T 232/249)

"When Jesus saw that many were having this crucifixion nightmare within their own private worlds, he decided to use their imaginary crucifixion as a teaching device, just as the Holy Spirit takes everything the ego has made and puts it to better use.

"But what's really important about all this," I told her, "is what we do about the crucifixion NOW. If you defend the false belief that Jesus WAS crucified, it means that you WANT him to be crucified now! Why else would you insist that he WAS crucified.

"The Course says that 'in the calm light of truth, let us recognize that you believe you have crucified God's Son. You have not admitted to this 'terrible' secret. Because you would still wish to crucify him if you can find him.'" (T 224/240)

"Jesus says that 'Perception is a wish fulfilled.' (T 515/554) In other words, what you are perceiving is what you would like TO BE true. If you perceive that Jesus WAS crucified, even 2000 years ago, then that is what you would like to be true NOW.

"Jesus can only come into your awareness and into your presence in your own mind NOW. He cannot come into a physical world 2000 years ago, because there is NO physical world 2000 years ago, and never was! The planet earth and the entire universe is a dream within your own mind. And in that dream, ONLY what you choose can occur.

"There is no actual historical, real solid crucifixion. In your private world you have the choice to have Jesus crucified, or NOT crucified. It's up to you. He can only be crucified in your own mind and nowhere else, since there is nowhere else. If you deny this, then it means that you are simply defending your ego against the truth. Jesus says that 'the dream of crucifixion still lies heavy on your eyes, but what you see in dreams is not reality. While you perceive the Son of God as crucified, you are asleep. And as long as you believe that you can crucify him, you are only having nightmares.' (T 194/209) In order to awaken, then, it is necessary to realize that: THERE IS NO CRUCIFIXION AND NEVER WAS!"

"But this is the complete opposite of what the world believes," my student said.

"Right. But then, *A Course In Miracles* says that 'the world will end when its thought system has been completely reversed.' (M 35/36) And the ending of the world is our resurrection. And so, Jesus asks us now, 'Would you join in the resurrection or the crucifixion?'" (T 192/207)

"You know," my student said, "I don't believe that Jesus was ever crucified. At least not in my world, nor in his."

"Nor in mine," I said.

Author, minister, and lecturer Harmon H. Bro, Ph.D., is critical of the teachings in ACIM. As a young man he witnessed about 700 Cayce readings. Several of the books he has written are in-depth studies of the Cayce work, especially as it relates to the teachings of Christianity. It is his assertion that much of the information in the Course is in opposition to the Cayce readings and Christianity, although other students of the Cayce readings find the ACIM material helpful.

According to Dr. Bro's interpretation and understanding of the concepts in the Course, Jesus states that "the earth itself is an illusion, again created by the separated ego; it could not have been created by God, because the Course's God is not capable of creating anything that is not eternal. Only minds are eternal and important. For them the Course is a divine gift of 'mind-training.'

"In this view, Cayce's thousands of medical readings, meant to help those who suffer, are wasted effort, except insofar as he may have taught them that bodies are illusion, in a collective dream of artificial separation from God."

Well, if there is a possibility the ACIM information is valid, then let's continue reading mind words printed with illusionary ink on illusionary paper!

Sometimes I think it is possible that well-known and frequently studied, respected, and quoted psychics—those that were not known as channels for information dispensed by some distinguished ethereal entity or spiritual hierarchy, but reached out into the different realms where they absorbed knowledge, or received visions for interpretation—that they at times attempted to force their data collection procedure too far (just as Edgar Cayce was at times into the "outer limits" of his power as described by his sons), an altitude too distant or high for their vibrational instrument. Perhaps their clairvoyant eyesight was blurred, or the interpretation of their experiences became confused.

Rudolph Steiner is well-known and respected as an author, philosopher, educator, and a person who had exceptional extrasensory abilities. He founded the Anthroposophical Society, which is still active in this country and others and has written books on different subjects, including many on his interpretation of the teachings in the Bible.

In his book *The Gospel of St. Luke, Lecture Five,* Rudolph

Steiner claims, respecting Jesus, that there were not one, but two—the Nathan Jesus and the Solomon Jesus!

For some reason I never felt attracted to the Steiner teachings. I had browsed through only a few Steiner books when the two-baby-Jesus teaching was enthusiastically explained to me by a Steiner supporter. The above book/lecture was recommended; which I read it and found it confusing, difficult, and, for me, unacceptable.

The entire text of Lecture Five is long and complicated. I have attempted to rearrange and excerpt a few passages I felt would be sufficient as a short introduction to the overall proposition without going into extensive detail:

> I shall say things today that are not found in the Gospels; but you will understand the Bible all the better if you learn from investigation of the Akashic Chronicle [the universal record]. . .The birth of the two Jesus children were separated by a period of a few months. . .Thus we see the two Jesus-children growing up. The son of Joseph and Mary of the Nathan line was born of a young mother. . .this couple continued to live in Nazareth with their son. They had no other children. When Joseph and Mary of the Solomon line returned with their son from Egypt, they settled in Nazareth, and as related in the Gospel of St. Mark, had several more children: Simon, Judas, Joseph, James and two sisters. . .Thus in the Nathan Jesus we see a Being with infinite depths of feeling, and in the Solomon Jesus an Individuality of exceptional maturity, having profound understanding of the world. . .The parents were in friendly relationships and the children grew up as near neighbors until they were about twelve years old. . .We will enquire of the imperishable Akashic Chronicle. . .The facts of existence are by no means simple. . .At a certain stage of development some individuality may need conditions different than those that were present at the beginning of life. Hence it repeatedly happens that someone lives to a certain age and then suddenly falls into a state of deathlike unconsciousness. A transformation takes place: his own Ego leaves him and another Ego passes into his bodily constitution [now known as *walk-ins*?]. . .In the case of the twelve-

year-old Jesus the following happened. The Ego of the [Solomon] Jesus. . .in order to reach the highest level of his epoch, left that body and passed into the body of the Nathan Jesus who then appeared as one transformed. His parents did not recognize him; nor did they understand his words. . .

If you were to read this entire lecture, I think you too would find it difficult and hard to understand. The passages I've excerpted are simply meant to add a little more to your awareness. To encourage you to be skeptical and discerning with all extrasensory information—but with an open mind.

Maurice Maeterlinck, who was awarded the Nobel Prize for Literature in 1911, wrote in the book *The Great Secret*: "Rudolph Steiner, who, when he does not lose himself in visions—plausible, perhaps, but incapable of verification—of prehistoric ages, of astral negatives, and of life on other planets, is a shrewd and accurate thinker. . ." In a later chapter, concerning Steiner, he states, ". . .we remind ourselves that the subconscious, which has already surprised us so often, may perhaps have in store for us further surprises which may be as fantastic as those of the Austrian theosophist; and, having learned prudence from experience, we refrain from condemning him without appeal."

The Steiner material and the ACIM teachings don't strike a note within me—they don't make sense or feel appropriate. However, I do feel we should try to keep in mind the situation that Dr. Ritchie wrote about—the books of the universe as they were being studied by the beings dressed in brown monkish robes in that enormous ethereal library in the fourth realm: "I became aware that the Christ was watching these souls in their study of the universe's religions and saw He did not judge any of them. They too were not judging the religions which they were studying but were interested in the many different ways the beings of the universe had attempted to come to understand their Creator."

Cayce was asked: "What is truth?" He answered:

That which makes aware of the Divine within each and every activity. . .and is a growth. . .that which makes aware to the inmost self or the soul the Divine and its purposes with that soul. (262-81)

Truth is growth. For what is truth today may be tomorrow only partially so, to a developing soul! (1297-1)

It was very unusual for Cayce to continue a reading once the conductor gave him the suggestion to return to is waking state of consciousness. But perhaps the people involved at the time were arguing over some philosophical or religious belief. For at the end of one reading, after he was given the suggestion for waking, he spontaneously offered the following:

Because many interpret that they have received contrary to thine own manner of thought, find ye not fault with them; for He has given, "They that gather not with us scatter abroad" that which may open the door, the way, for those that seek to know the Maker, the Giver of Life, eternal. (254-78)

Finally, there is a difference between the "Grail Message" and the Edgar Cayce readings concerning interpretation, or the perception, of the immaculate conception of the Virgin Mary, the mother of Jesus. The "Grail Message" is emphatic that this was not possible because it would be in opposition to Natural Law. Actually, the Cayce readings are the only source I've encountered that claims it was Natural Law. On the subject the readings state:

. . .And this [the immaculate conception] is a stumblingstone to many of the wordly-wise. (5749-15)

Q: Is the teaching of the Roman Catholic Church correct, in that Mary was without original sin from the moment of her conception in the womb of Anne [Mary's mother]?
A: It would be correct in any case. Correct more in this. For as from the material teaching of that just referred to, you see, in the beginning, Mary was the twin Soul of the Master in the entrance into the earth.
Q: Was Anne also prepared for her part as the mother of Mary?
A: Only in general, not as specific as Mary. . .there was no belief in the fact that Anne proclaimed that the child was without father. Its like many proclaiming today that the

Master was immaculately conceived; they say, "Impossible!" They say it isn't in compliance with the natural law. IT IS NATURAL LAW, as has been indicated by the projection of mind into matter. . .as did man [souls at the beginning of their earth cycle of development].

Q: Then neither Mary nor Jesus had a human father?

A: Neither Mary nor Jesus had a human father. They were one soul so far as the earth is concerned." (5749-8)

As I hope I've demonstrated by now, there are many matters that need to be taken into consideration when dealing with what is broadly termed "metaphysical information."

Even the practice of meditation should be approached with extreme caution and preparation. It is much different than prayer. Just as Edgar Evans Cayce urged everyone to first read the chapter on "The Nature of Psychic Perception" in *The Outer Limits of Edgar Cayce's Power* before researching the Cayce readings, I would urge everyone to read *Venture Inward* before attempting meditation. With prayer you are the one doing the communicating. With meditation, one needs to fully understand the dangers involved as well as the benefits. For it is the attempt to invite the Spirit within to do the communicating. However, as we've seen, there are unsavory spirit entities anxious to plug their extension cord into your circuitry!

The Cayce readings claim that meditation is an opening of the endocrine glands of the physical body, sometimes known as the spiritual centers. This creates the conditions by which it's possible for communication to take place. The practice of certain methods of yoga create the same effect.

In readings on the subject of yoga, we find:

Then WHO and WHAT would the entity have to direct self in such experiences? To be loosed without a governor, or a director, may easily become harmful. (2475-1)

The body is a supersensitive individual who has allowed itself—through study—through opening the gland centers of the body, to become possessed with activities outside of itself. . .

Q: How did I happen to pick this up?

A: The body—in its study, opened the gland centers, and allowed self to become sensitive to outside influences.

Q: What is it exactly that assails me?

A: Outside influences. Disincarnate entities. (5221-1)

In another reading we find that, should the wrong purposes or goals, those for material gain only, be the intent of a person attempting to open the glands or spiritual centers, the person would eventually become a "Frankenstein." (262-20)

As to the benefits of meditation, there are many:

Q: Is it possible to meditate and obtain needed information?

A: On any subject. Whether you are going digging for fishing worms, or playing a concerto! (1861-12)

Along with the warnings in the readings on meditation, there are specific details, methods, advice, and suggestions for getting started. The book *Meditation and the Mind of Man* by Herbert B. Puryear, Ph.D., and Mark A. Thurston, Ph.D., is an excellent guide. There are many others. So, as the saying goes, "forewarned is forearmed."

Consider! If you can get in trouble when attempting to communicate with the Holy Spirit, what are the dangers with satanic practices that are conscious attempts to communicate with the Devil? We already know the havoc the Ouija board and automatic writing can wreak. Stepping up to the Devil's ticket counter could easily result in you becoming the holder of a one-way ticket to the insane asylum—or worse—that place known as Hell!

And beware of all "psychics" who are anxious to offer advice and counsel; Hugh Lynn Cayce was extremely wary of all psychics, and he knew many. There are very few that have been investigated, researched, and documented. All one has to do to open a shop in the psychic business is hang out a shingle. They may be sincere in their efforts, but they can still be wrong. I know of only a handful that I would take seriously. And of this number, each and every one will readily admit they can make mistakes.

We've pretty much covered the source and interpretation

scenario in this chapter—the problems and differences in opinions and conclusions concerning psychic information.

Undoubtedly there are differences of opinion and conclusions among researchers and students of the Bible. The same applies to the Edgar Cayce readings and other metaphysical material. And sometimes the debates are intense and heated ones!

There are disputes concerning the earth changes predictions and, more specifically, estimations regarding the severity and form in which they will be expressed. Will it be volcanic eruptions, earthquakes, strange weather patterns, strife, wars, turmoil, disease, famine, economic problems, ecological disasters, and so forth.

Will it be all, none, or just some of the above? No one knows, but as with any opinion, interpretation, or conclusion, don't take another's word for it. Ask any and every person who has a theory or belief, and is trying to convince others of the answers, for explicit evidence, references, and the reasoning applied in arriving at conclusions. Just as you should do with the information I've written here.

Furthermore, attempt to discover any altered facts, or find material facts that, because of poor research or other reasons, have been omitted. With all of this, there may be ulterior motives or hidden agendas involved.

If these changes are now inevitable, as some believe, then the best approach we can take is to do everything in our power to lessen the severity. Each person can make a difference—a better world for all of humanity.

Where Do We Go From Here?

In 1932, during the depths of the Great Depression, Edgar Cayce gave a reading on "Present World Conditions." I'd like to include an excerpt from this reading as we near the end of this correspondence; it's as appropriate today as it was then:

With the present conditions, then, that exist—these have all come to that place in the development of the human family where there must be a reckoning, a one point upon which all can agree, that out of all of this turmoil that has arisen from the social life, racial differences, the outlook [of religious convictions and doctrine] upon the relationship of man to the Creative Forces or his God, and his relationships one with another, must come to some COMMON basis upon which all may agree. You say at once such a thing is impractical, impossible! What has caused the present conditions, not alone at home, but abroad? It is that realization that was asked some thousands of years ago, "Where IS thy brother? His blood CRIES to me from the ground!" and the other portion of the world has answered, IS answering, "Am I my brother's keeper?" The world, AS a world—that makes for the disruption, for the discontent— has lost its ideal. Man may not have the same IDEA. Man—ALL men—may have the same IDEAL.

As the Spirit of God once moved to bring peace and harmony out of Chaos, so must the Spirit move over the earth and magnify itself in the hearts, minds and souls of men to bring peace, harmony and understanding, that they may dwell together in a way that will bring peace, that harmony, that can only come with all having the one ideal; not the one idea, but "Thou shalt love the Lord thy God with all thine heart, thy neighbor AS thyself." This is the whole Law, this is the whole answer to the world, to each and every soul. That is the answer to the world conditions as they exist today.

How shall this be brought about? As each in their own respective sphere [their daily lives] put into action that they know to be the fulfilling of that [quoted above] as has been from the beginning. . .Man's answer to everything has been POWER—Power of money, Power of position, Power of wealth, Power of this, that or the other. This has NEVER been GOD'S way, will never be God's way. Rather little by little, line upon line, here a little, there a little, each thinking rather of the other. . . (3976-8)

We can all change for the better if we want to. We'll make mistakes, but we have to keep trying. That's why we were placed in this school known as Planet Earth. Somehow, some way, by going to the classes and learning the lessons of life, we discover the many activities and forms that demonstrate God's love for all souls.

We find an example of God's love, demonstrated in the form we know as forgiveness, in Paul's letter to Timothy (1-1:15-16):

Here are words you may trust, words that merit full acceptance: "Christ Jesus came into the world to save sinners"; and among them I stand first. But I was mercifully dealt with for this very purpose, that Jesus Christ might find in me the first occasion for displaying all His patience, and that I might be typical of all who were in future to have faith in Him and gain eternal life.

So I suppose if Paul was first in the "sinner's line" that has been forming on earth for all these years, and he was dealt with mercifully, we may all have a chance! All we have to do is take that first step on the *Love* stairWay to eternity. The one with *Forgive* etched in the first stone tread.

A Poem For Amy

This is the voyage of AMY BETH'S SOUL,
Born long ago with a wonderful GOAL.

GOD was alone, *and* HE longed for a "WE,"
To be FATHER and MOTHER of a great family.

For GOD's not a "HE" nor a "SHE" nor a "IT,"
In truth GOD's all these and with no favorite.

But it's been allowed throughout ages and ages,
That GOD's "HE" or "HIM" for speech and for pages.

"GOD is LOVE, GOD is LAW," GOD's always the same,
And HIS "SPIRIT" is "LIFE"—an unquenchable flame.

And because GOD is LOVE HE wanted to share,
So HE ordained a PLAN and called it "AWARE."

Then like sparks from a volcano exploding apart,
Showers of SPIRITS soared out from GOD'S heart.

And one of those SPIRITS had Amy's name in it,
But she still needed TOOLS to work in GOD'S INFINITE.

So GOD gave Amy's SPIRIT two wondrous TOOLS,
A *MIND* and *FREE WILL* to master GOD'S RULES.

She was now ordained "SOUL" and prepared to begin,
She could *THINK*, she could *CHOOSE*, ETERNAL SPIRIT within.

And GOD made the LAWS for the World and the SOULS,
So Amy's and others could all play their roles.

SOULS had bodies transparent that are known as "ethereal,"
To move freely in the Universe without gravity material.

GOD wanted each SOUL to know it was special,
To see all HIS Worlds like Angels celestial.

Amy's SOUL was to learn in its own unique way,
To return as GOD's friend and not go astray.

So into GOD'S World Amy's SOUL went a flying,
To learn about LOVE after trying and trying.

At first it was easy with so much to see,
From planets to stars to the great galaxy.

As Amy's SOUL gazed around, she saw something new,
Mother earth in her splendorous, radiant blue.

Soon Her SOUL and others chose to play a new game,
In the water, the air, the dirt and the flame.

They felt what it was to be cooled by the breeze,
To sense all the creatures with a care free ease.

And GOD said "please stop, before its too late,"
But the SOULS said "what for, this must be our fate!"

"Very well," GOD replied, "you may do as you choose,
But remember this warning, your SOUL you could lose."

Now the SOULS at this time were so young and so new,
They didn't have names and their group wasn't two.

The SOULS could play god for they had a new toy,
But soon they would choose to be girl or be boy.

One of the SOUL'S rules from the very first hour,
"No dwelling in animals, not even a dinosaur!"

For the SOUL of each Human is a world in itself,
Its different for horses, or even an elf.

Each species of animals has a "group soul" for its own,
They're part of GOD's plan to help our SOULS become grown.

So SOULS fashioned earth bodies and gave themselves names,
The better to craft and to play earth-type games.

Skin color became part of each maiden and fellow,
Some black, some brown, or red, white or yellow.

GOD hoped that each SOUL would love all the others,
Be helpful and caring to their sisters and brothers.

When launched from GOD'S heart she was light as a feather,
But now Amy's SOUL started feeling much heavier.

Amy's reason for being was becoming less clear,
Her earth body's mind caught a glimmer of fear.

GOD said "don't worry, you've MY SPIRIT within,
You can grow in the earth and not take one aspirin."

"My LOVE will protect you, take care of your needs,
You're meant to serve others, so start planting seeds."

"For the seed of an apple when planted by ME,
Will give forth much fruit from a beautiful tree."

"The seeds that you plant are your *thoughts*, *words* and *deeds*,
You can help create flowers or just create weeds."

"Its all up to you for I gave you *FREE WILL*,
Your SOUL can be healthy or it can be ill."

GOD hopes that each SOUL will learn how to LOVE,
To return to GOD'S hands with a fit like a glove.

And because each SOUL'S expression from others is different,
Each may play in GOD'S band with its unique SOUL instrument.

Each SOUL then becomes like a daughter and son,
To help GOD with CREATION and have lots of fun.

The SOULS thought "how simple," we each have our task,
Then something went wrong, "what could that be?" you ask.

The SOUL'S earth body you know has many a need,
It must sleep, it must eat, and hopefully not bleed.

And when SOULS began planting, something new would crop up,
Desire for more than just shelter and a full cup.

SOULS were called Humans when dwelling in earth bodies,
And they could be goodies or they could be naughties.

Now a funny thing happened, the more toys Humans had,
The more toys they wanted to make them feel glad.

And GOD'S promise to SOULS to them became dimmer,
They now were not sure HE'd provide them with dinner.

"Fear *of lack*" was intruding with GOD'S lasting LOVE,
And the children of GOD would now push and now shove.

And if a brother or sister had things they did not,
Some were jealous and angry, and sometimes they fought.

And because of GOD'S LAWS, SOULS started to suffer,
What they served up to others would *return* as their supper.

From one of GOD'S LAWS there can be no distraction,
"For every single action there's an equal reaction."

From the very beginning GOD'S LAWS could not change,
But HIS patience gives SOULS time to roam HIS great range.

For reincarnation, a belief most Humans accept,
Is an expression of GOD'S patience for SOULS gone inept.

When a SOUL left its earth body it would go to GOD'S heavens,
Visit worlds and the planets, then return for earth lessons.

SOULS could wander GOD'S UNIVERSE, attend different schools,
Then choose a new earth body to be bright or be fools.

They would choose Mom and Dad whom they'd known in the past,
And their family and relationships from a past telecast.

The *thought, word,* and *deed* seeds in other lives sown,
The SOUL would now harvest for happy or moan.

So you can't blame others when for you things go bad,
But you can pat your own back for the good luck you've had.

SOULS have to correct any harm they have done,
Before joining GOD to have all that fun.

Now on planet earth there were five separate races,
So SOULS could grow LOVE in all kinds of places.

Each race had its wisdom and SOULS could try all,
Living with the sand or the snow or hot tropical.

And if a SOUL disliked others because of their shade,
In a future life it would join that same race unafraid.

So don't condemn others whatever the reason,
For you're judging yourself from some other season.

For that which you hate of the SOUL becomes part,
You must learn to have faith and to clean out your heart.

A new partner joined "fear" that we all know as "greed,"
And many a Human on these two traits it would feed.

"Fear" and "greed" were soon joined by one more polluter,
Some Humans wanted "power" for another wrong tutor.

So the fate all the SOULS long ago thought was right,
Brought problems and pain as part of their plight.

By now all the Humans had two MINDS in their head,
The awake mind, and the SOUL MIND (more alert when in bed).

The awake mind and the SOUL MIND should equally work,
The SOUL MIND to restrain Humans from being a jerk.

When Humans wear out after living in earth's hemispheres,
Both Minds become one MIND to absorb all SOUL'S yesteryears.

For with GOD there's no time, there's only eternity,
Its only on Earth clocks enjoy popularity.

And the SPIRIT of GOD was still lodged in each SOUL,
But most Humans ignored it as they danced rock and roll.

So Amy's SOUL and most others were now feeling lost,
Like ships with no rudders, they were heaved, they were tossed.

SOULS remembered GOD'S warning to not go astray,
If they didn't learn LOVE they could start to decay.

Remember GOD'S plan, the one called "AWARE,"
That GOD wanted friends with whom HE could share.

But true friends must be free to say "yes" or say "no,"
That's why the *FREE WILL,* SOULS could come, they could go.

If GOD was domineering, SOULS wouldn't have fun,
And that's no way to treat a daughter or son.

GOD wants every SOUL to be an "AWARE INDIVIDUAL,"
To be part of HIS everything and become "wHoly" visional.

He wants you to make your WILL one with HIS,
An actor on HIS stage of CREATION'S show biz.

This is the HEAVEN where your SOUL's meant to dwell,
But "what then," you might ask, "is that place known as HELL?"

Deep down we all know LOVE's a two way street,
And to walk down LOVE'S road you must use your feet.

There's a straight road, you know, and many others that bend,
The one that you travel will determine SOUL'S end.

Feed your SOUL only garbage, and it starts to be ill,
The SOUL'S MIND slowly *dulls* from wrong use of *FREE WILL.*

And your friends and acquaintances that are attracted to you,
Will help you play sewage and they'll like garbage too.

If you act like a hog with the "birds and the bees,"
Though they're here for a purpose, pigs can attract fleas.

If sex and violence are entertainment's main course meal,
The message they portray may be tomorrow's newsreel.

The earth and ethereal bodies slide together like a telescopes'
You can focus to view classics or just watch the soaps.

Thoughts, words and deeds are your ethereal energy,
Like an electrical magnet it will attract your SOUL'S destiny.

And GOD'S LAWS work the same when you're in the beyond,
You'll hang out with "like" SOULS and to them you will bond.

Imagine living in a mansion with all SOULS just like you,
Then you'll see your real self, it'll be through and through.

And if you're miserable here and take your own life,
You've short circuited SOUL'S plan to deal with the strife.

You'll find yourself "over there" disoriented and alone,
Aimlessly wandering, and with no friends to phone.

And then you'll return to face the same difficulties again,
Don't run from your problems, they're part of SOUL'S regimen.

Most religions teach that suicide's a selfish act,
Instead of adding to SOUL'S growth, to commit is subtract.

And don't harm another for that prized toy that you want,
Any crime you commit becomes your SOUL'S prison haunt.

Don't comply with GOD'S LAWS and one day you could find,
As the old saying goes, "you could lose your MIND."

A SOUL MIND that contains *wrong* AWARENESS and that's *all,*
The SOUL'S SPIRIT will blot out, they'll be nothing to recall.

And the AWARE INDIVIDUAL GOD wants you to be,
Will not come to pass without memory.

Then you can't be an actor on CREATION'S great stage,
Because remembering your lines is how you engage.

That's the SOUL'S HELL that perchance could take place,
To return to GOD'S theater with the SPIRIT but a blank face.

The SOUL'S ETERNAL SPIRIT, the one GOD gave two TOOLS,
Returns empty handed because it didn't follow GOD'S RULES.

GOD'S GRACE and HIS LOVE are bestowed on SOULS freely,
But SOULS must *choose* GOD'S WAY like the Man from Galilee.

Some say this is the true meaning of the "New Age,"
That SOULS must choose GOD'S WAY or confront "diseng*Age.*"

And because of GOD'S LAWS there cannot be exceptions,
In GOD'S eyes SOULS are equal, even with their imperfections.

The last thing GOD wants is for SOULS to HELL happen,
So on each SOUL's heart HIS LAWS keep a rappin'.

That's why "long-suffering" is one fruit of SOUL'S SPIRIT,
It speaks from GOD'S LAWS, the SOUL hopefully to hear it.

Even GOD'S insects will find windows light,
While some humans it seems can't tell the day from the night.

Ants march to GOD'S orders whether day or the night,
Your honey they'll find with their GOD-given radar sight.

And remember that apple on GOD'S beautiful tree,
It too has to ripen with its GOD-given memory.

If it rots on the tree and falls with a thud,
Only seeds will survive to return to GOD'S mud.

Mother Natures great bounty, the vegetables and fruit,
Each have there own schedule to mature absolute.

SOULS can't forever wander like the mythical salamander,
Someday SOULS must graduate as marked on GOD'S calendar.

But don't think you can "catch up" because you can cram,
Your words, thoughts and deeds are a book, not a telegram.

You can't force your SOUL'S growth like a hot house tomato,
And you won't have much worth as a dirt-bound couch potato.

So this is GOD'S SYSTEM where we breathe and we live,
But the DOCTOR's diagnosed Humans may need a laxative!

If a vast number of SOULS all decide to play hooky,
To wash in the slop and get their hands gooky.

They start to flunk classes in GOD'S temple schools,
So HE sends SOULS new tests to remind them HIS RULES.

And sometimes these tests must be difficult and hard,
But if SOULS start to drown they need a lifeguard.

For we all know to swim we cannot cease our motion,
Or we'll be swallowed up like a drop in GOD'S ocean.

So its GOD to the rescue on today's calendar page,
Its time for the "changes" to birth the *New Age*.

For we can't go on treating our planet like this,
Our poor Mother Earth will soon need dialysis.

Mother Earth knows that she's slowly dying,
From abuse and neglect She's started crying.

Mother's beginning to feel dizzy, to be out of balance,
She must stop the bleeding, or She won't hold Her silence.

And like a Mother Superior she can be very strict,
She can cause withdrawal pains for the Human addict.

And each SOUL MIND's aware Mother knows best,
But try warning the earth mind, even when its at rest.

So many toys and amusements Humans believe they all need,
May run out of gas, then they'll wish for a steed.

And even the basics like food, clothing and shelter,
Need Mother Earth's blessing, to prevent helter-skelter.

So Mother's now broadcasting for Humans to be knowing,
And to get their attention many strong winds She's a'blowing.

And She has other ways so we stop causing Her aches,
She'll erupt some volcanos and shake us some earthquakes.

Mother has many a means in Her bag of tricks,
To break our bad habits and take away our fix.

She's reluctant to sit on the court of last resort,
But what else can She do Human actions to thwart?

The wars and pollution, the greed and the hate,
All have to be stopped before it's too late.

And remember the races that each had a wisdom,
Religions also have wisdom from Judaism to Islam.

It won't help to be prejudice towards a religion or race,
You've most likely been a member, and yourself you deface.

Each SOUL has to grow in its own special way,
So it attends various "Churches" to learn what it may.

And what of great teachers with their spiritual bread,
Like Buddah and Moses and ALLAH'S Mohammed.

Many have ignored their pleas and their call,
Conflicts abound in the home, streets and school hall.

GOD even sent HIS SON if you choose to believe,
To celebrate His birth the day after Christmas Eve.

And Jesus worked hard to show us the WAY,
Sacrificing His life to save SOULS gone astray.

The SOUL of Jesus Christ is WHOLE and AWARE,
He's there for the asking, our burdens to help bear.

Some say our present world resembles John's vision of Babylon,
And that John's TV weather man forecast Armageddon.

That this Age was foretold, *right* from *wrong* would be *blurred,*
Warned to change or be ashes for the Phoenix Firebird.

Even word usage is mixed up, or so it would appear,
"Bad" is "good," "lust" is "love," "to die for" is not clear.

And as we watch world events unfold in the news,
Conflicts and killing, starvation, then—"take a cruise."

So the curtain's gone up, it's "showtime" for Planet Earth,
Amy's SOUL and all others the New Age they must birth.

They can plow under the field and bury the bad weeds,
To influence the "changes" with good thoughts, words and deeds.

The next "Age" that's promised will be beautiful—no sleaze,
The birth pangs that accompany it we can each help to ease.

It's all up to us, we must LOVE and FORGIVE,
To return to GOD'S arms, AWARE and to LIVE.

Unfortunately if poets reach the pearly gates with just words,
They'll be laughed out of town to GOD'S land of the absurds.

And if for this poet the grim reaper from GOD's sent,
Please, not yet!

More time's needed to change and repent!

Bibliography

Abd-Ru-Shin. *In the Light of Truth.* Stuttgart: Stiftung Gralsbotschaft Publishing Company, Stuttgart, 1971.

Ad Astra. "Lookout for Planet X. (search for a tenth planet)." *Ad Astra*, March 1990: 5.

The American Heritage Dictionary. New York: American Heritage Publishing Co., Inc., and Houghton Mifflin Company, 1969.

Baigent, Michael, and Richard Leigh. *The Dead Sea Scrolls Deception.* New York: Summit Books, 1991.

Berlitz, Charles. *Doomsday, 1999 A.D.* New York: Doubleday and Company, New York, 1981.

Brinkley, Danion: Video tape available from The Eclectic Viewpoint, P.O. Box 802735, Dallas, TX 75380.

Cayce, Edgar Evans, and Hugh Lynn Cayce. *The Outer Limits of Edgar Cayce's Power.* New York: Harper and Row, 1971.

Cayce, Hugh Lynn. *Earth Changes Update.* Vriginia Beach, VA: A.R.E. Press, 1980.

_____. *Venture Inward,* New York: Harper and Row, 1964.

Cerminara, Gina, Ph.D. *Many Mansions.* New York: William Morrow and Company, 1967.

Cheetham, Erika. *The Man Who Saw Tomorrow.* New York: Berkley Books, 1981.

Portions from *A Course In Miracles*, © 1975. Reprinted by permission of the Foundation for Inner Peace, PO Box 1104, Glen Ellen, CA 95442.

Dupont, Yves. *Catholic Prophecy, The Coming Chastisement*. Rockford, IL: Tan Books and Publishers, 1970.

Fisher, Joe. *The Case For Reincarnation*. Toronto: William Collins Sons, 1984.

Furst, Jeffrey. *Edgar Cayce's Story of Jesus*. New York: Coward-McCann, Inc., 1968.

Gospel of St. Luke. Rudolph Steiner Publications, London, 1935.

Hall, Manly Palmer. The Secret Destiny of America. New York: Philosophical Library, 1944.

Head, Joseph, and S.L. Cranston. *Reincarnation, An East West Anthology*. Wheaton, IL: Quest Books, 1967.

_____. *Reincarnation in World Thought*. New York: Julian Press, 1967.

Hieronimus, Robert, Ph.D. *America's Secret Destiny*. Rochester, NY: Destiny Books, 1989.

Insight Newsletter, P.O. Box 391, Gangies, BC.

Jochmans, J.R. *Rolling Thunder, The Coming Earth Changes*. Albuquerque, NM: Sun Publishing Company, Albuquerque, NM, 1980.

Littman, Mark. "Where is Planet X?" *Sky and Telescope*, Dec. 1989: 596-600.

MacLaine, Shirley. *Out On a Limb*. New York: Bantam Books, 1983.

MacGregor, Geddes. *Reincarnation on Christianity*. Wheaton, IL: The Theosophical Publishing House, 1986.

Maeterlink, Maurice. *The Great Secret*. New York: University Books, Inc. (Carol Publishing Co.), 1969.

Mallin, Jay. "Beyond Pluto: Planet X Search Gets Warmer." Washington *Times*, April 1990: 11.

Marbach, William D. "The Search for Planet X." *Newsweek*, July 1987:55.

Moody, Raymond A., Jr., M.D., Ph.D. *Life After Life*. Covington, GA: Mockingbird Books, 1975.

Nelson, Kirk. *The Second Coming*. Vriginia Beach, VA: Wright Publishing Company, 1986.

The New English Bible. Oxford University Press, Cambridge University Press, 1970.

Puryear, Herbert Bruce. *Why Jesus Taught Reincarnation*. Scottsdale, AZ: New Paradigm Press, 1992.

Puryear, Herbert B., Ph.D., and Mark Thurston, Ph.D. *Meditation and the Mind of Man*. Virginia Beach, VA: A.R.E. Press, 1975.

Reilly, Harold J., with Ruth Hagy Brod. *The Edgar Cayce Handbook for Health Through Drugless Therapy*. New York: MacMillan, 1975.

Ritchie, George G., M.D. *My Life After Dying*. Norfolk, VA: Hampton Roads Publishing Co., Inc., 1991.

Scallion, Gordon-Michael. Earth Changes Report. Available from the Matrix Institute, P.O. Box 87, Westmoreland, N.H. 03467.

Seeds, Michael A. *Foundations of Astronomy*. Belmont: Wadsworth Publishing Company, 1990.

Sitchin, Zecharia. *The 12th Planet*. New York: Stein and Day, 1976.

_____. *Genesis Revisited*. New York: Avon Books, 1990.

Stearn, Jess. *The Sleeping Prophet*. New York: Doubleday, 1967.

Steinbach, Dr. Richard. *How Is It That We Live After Death and What Is The Meaning Of Life*. Stuttgart: Stiftung Gralsbotschaft Publishing Company, 1980.

Stover, Dawn. "The Tenth Planet." *Popular Science*, Nov. 1991: 25.

Sugrue, Thomas. *There is a River*. New York: Holt, Rinehart, & Winston, 1942.

Timms, Moira. *Prophecies and Predictions*. Santz Cruz, CA: Unity Press, 1980.

_____. *Beyond Prophecies and Predictions*. New York: Ballantine Books, 1994.

Tombaugh, Clyde W. "Plates, Pluto, and Planets X." *Sky and Telescope*, April 1991: 360-361.

Weisburd, Stefi. "Planet X and the Killer Comets." *Science News*, Jan. 1987: 40-41.

Weiss, Brian L., M.D. *Through Time Into Healing*. New York: Simon and Schuster, 1992.

Whitton, Joel L., M.D., Ph.D., and Joe Fisher. *Life Between Life,* New York: Doubleday and Company, 1986.

The Wisdom Of Ramala, Essex, England: C.W. Daniel Company Limited, 1986.

Woodward, Mary Ann. *Edgar Cayce's Story of Karma*. New York: Coward-McCann, Inc., 1971.

Other Books for Your Consideration

1. Aron Abrahamson. *On Wings of Spirit*. Virginia Beach, VA: A.R.E. Press, 1993.

2. Sidney Farr. *What Tom Sawyer Learned from Dying*. Norfolk, VA: Hampton Roads Publishing Co., 1993.

3. J. Edwin Carter. *Living Is Forever*. Norfolk, VA: Hampton Roads Publishing Co., 1990.

4. Hugh Lynn Cayce. *Faces of Fear*. New York: Harper and Row, 1980.

5. Sun Bear with Wabun Wind. *Black Dawn, Bright Day*. New York: Simon & Schuster (Fireside Books), 1992.

6. Bruce McArthur. *Your Life, Why It Is the Way It Is, and What You Can Do About It*. Virginia Beach, VA: A.R.E. Press, 1993.

7. Jess Stearn. *Intimates Through Time*. New York: Harper & Row, 1976.

8. Mary Summer Rain. *Phoenix Rising*. Norfolk, VA.: Hampton Roads Publishing Co., 1993.

About the Cover Artist

Francine Barbet began her career as a commercial artist in New York, where her work appeared in *The New York Times* magazine and on greeting cards of several companies. She turned to decorating services as an accomodation to her role as a parent, working with top decorators on wall and furniture designs.

She currently works with oil and water colors, and her art focuses on angels, children, and the preservation of natural life. Her numerous paintings of angels on windows and canvas have a mystical quality. She lives in Virginia Beach, Virginia, where she is known as The Angel Lady of the area.

She was recently commissioned by the Children's Hospital of the King's Daughters in Norfolk, Virginia, and her illustrations regularly appear in the international publication *Venture Inward*.